Where the Rubber Meets the Road

Denny Bucher

Published by JR Thomas, 2018.

WHERE THE RUBBER MEETS THE ROAD

First edition. March 10, 2018.

Copyright © 2018 Denny Bucher.

Written by Denny Bucher.

FOREWARD

I was attending a weekend men's retreat at the Billy Graham training center in Ashville, North Carolina when the guest speaker asked a very interesting question. He asked us to raise our hands if we had any detailed information about the life of our great grandparents. I don't think a single man raised his hand. He commented that it was sad that we knew so little about our ancestors, and challenged us to change that.

I took the challenge!

I contacted a number of elderly relatives and asked them questions about their parents and grandparents. I am so glad that I did as they have all since passed away since I interviewed them.

I hope you find this book interesting - I had a lot of fun writing it and I learned much about my heritage.

I would like to thank my wife Diann for her encouragement and her help with detail. My daughter Stephanie gave me a number of suggestions about events that I had left out.

Lastly, I want to thank Dick Thomas for his help in editing and putting it together.

Hope you enjoy it!

CHAPTER 1

I was born on December 11, 1942, at Porter Memorial Hospital in Valparaiso Indiana, the first child of Arthur Harry Bucher and Esther Levene Heiniger Bucher. Following me was my sister Suzanne, July 23, 1946, my brother Arden, August 29, 1948, my sister Laurie, September 17, 1952, and my brother Brian Timothy, February 10, 1956. I was very fortunate to have my grandparents in my life during my growing up years, and I have fond memories of all four of them. I was blessed by the fact that they all were strong committed Christians, and that commitment was the central part of their lives.

All of my ancestors came to the United States in the late 1800's from a small area in Western Europe. My grandfather on my father's side was Albert Bucher, and his father Gustov came from what was then Germany, specifically Alcese Lorrain. Today that area is part of France. He certainly did not consider himself French, but German. My Mom's father was Andrew Heiniger, and his family came from a small village in northern Switzerland, near the German border, Durrenroth.

While I do not know precisely where my Grandmothers were from, I am told that their families came from Germany's Rhine Valley. My father's mom was Marie Stortz and my mom's mother was Magdalena Heinold. They were all from a farming background, and their parents settled near a small town in Illinois near Peoria called Gridley. Gridley was almost totally settled by German immigrants, most of them farmers who came to the U.S. for opportunity and to avoid the religious persecution that was prevalent at that time. My Uncle Elmer told me that as a young man, my great grandfather Gustov had a job in his homeland where he walked four miles to and from work. After a long days work his pay was the amount of wood he could carry home!

My father, Arthur Harry Bucher was born on August 29, 1917 in Gridley. He told me that when he started school in 1923, he knew no English, even though he was born in Illinois. Grandpa Bert told me that he remembered going to church one Sunday soon after the start of World War I. Someone unknown had tacked a handwritten sign on the front door of the church that said, "There will be no German spoken here." He told me that the preacher gave a very short sermon in English. From that time on, English was the language of the Buchers. In fact, none of my Bucher or Heiniger ancestors had even a hint of a German accent when they spoke. My father could say a few things in German but had "lost" his knowledge of the German language as a result of not using it.

SOMETIME IN THE EARLY 1920's, my granddad's father Gustov got word of rich farmland at a bargain price in Indiana, about seventy five miles south east of Chicago. Because of the lands close location to the Kankakee River, constant flooding made the land hard to farm. Sometime during the early 1900's the Army Corps of Engineers straightened the river and dug a series of ditches that enabled the fields to be tiled and thus farmable. Grandfather Albert Bucher told me that his father, my great grandfather heard about the land in Indiana from a realtor who told them that they could sell their farm in Illinois and buy two in Indiana for the same amount. So, he sold his land in Illinois and made the move to Indiana. He told me that the land in Indiana was purchased for about half the cost of Illinois land. Since Gustov had several sons, he decided to buy two farms in Indiana and finance twenty five percent of the purchase. By the Late 1920's he had lost both farms and he died broke. As a result my grandfather Bert was very skeptical of any type of debt. Until he bought the farm that my uncle Ken now owns, he farmed for many years as a tenant farmer.

My uncle Vernon was the oldest child, my father Arthur was second born and twelve more brothers and sisters were born after him. One was stillborn and one survived for only a few days. Today, only my uncle Ken, the youngest survives. The other thirteen are deceased. Several died of natural causes at a young age. Aldene and Dwight died in accidents. My Dad, Arthur died at age fifty eight of cancer of the pancreas. Vernon, Imogene and Edith died in their late years of natural causes. Ella also lived to an old age and died from Alzheimer's. Elmer, Merle and Les died of natural causes late in life. All twelve of Bert and Marie's children who lived to adulthood, married and had children. I have sixty-three first cousins.

Several stories that my Dad or granddad told me are worth repeating. The first involved Harry Bucher, my granddad's brother. The Buchers were members of the Apostolic Christian Church. From the earliest days of the U.S.A. until 1973 conscription was the law of the land. While it changed several times, during most of the history of the USA, every young man was and is required to register for selective service at age eighteen. One of the beliefs of the Apostolic Christian Church is that since one of the Ten Commandments is "Do not kill"; members of the church should not bear arms. They were known as conscientious objectors. Some denominations such as Mennonites served in what was known as alternative service, spending their "military time" working in government hospitals, mental hospitals etc. Uncle Harry was drafted into the U.S. Army, but after arriving in boot camp he made it known that he would not be willing to shoot a rifle or any other weapon. This did not make his leaders happy and for some time he was ordered to march for hours with two cement blocks attached to a rope over his shoulder. When they finally determined that he would not change his position, he was allowed to serve in some capacity other than combat. Sometime later, the Military allowed anyone who was a conscientious objector to serve as a medic or do other duties that did not require arms. Many who served in this capacity were heroes in World War II, Korea and Vietnam. My brother Ardie served as a medic during his time in the Army. I will give more about my service later.

The Bucher family had a hard, but happy existence. They settled near the town of La Crosse, Indiana and were dairy farmers. Several tragedies occurred during the years before I was born. During the time the family was living on a farm north of La Crosse, the family farmhouse burned to the ground. Grandpa was in the field working when he saw smoke in the distance. He hurried home only to find the house was on fire and he could do nothing but watch it burn. He asked if anyone had saved his desk with all his important papers and when he was told no, he went into the house alone and dragged it out. I am not sure how many children were home at the time, but they lost everything except the clothes they were wearing. Handouts and help from the members of their church got them through this very tough time. They were able to rent a house at the edge of the farm for a while until they got another farm.

When Dad was a teenager, the Bucher family had grown to total about ten, which made it impossible for all to go anywhere together. While the Bucher family never failed to attend church on Sunday, about half of the kids would stay home each Sunday since there were too many to fit in the car. That meant several hours of unsupervised time. With no TV or Radio or other electric gadgets to keep them busy, they often turned to activities that would not have happened if Grandpa had been home. One of those was racing horses with buggies behind. I don't remember the details, but at least once this activity did not have a happy ending.

Raising twelve kids during the depression was undoubtedly a very difficult task for Grandpa and Grandma. Dad told me that he had to put cardboard in his shoes when the holes in the bottom wore through. He also used paraffin wax to fill the cavities in his teeth so the pain would be tolerable. As adults, both my mom and Dad had all of their teeth removed and fitted with dentures.

One of my favorite stories was that of my dad's education. After he completed the tenth grade and reached age sixteen, his father told him it was time to quit school and get a job. This was in 1933, during the worst of the depression. He quit school and worked at a variety of jobs during the next few years. He worked for local farmers, worked as a laborer on the railroad, worked in a grain elevator and worked for a butcher. He also worked for a short time as a bill collector. Interestingly, I also was a collector during my first couple of years with Firestone.

While working on the railroad he drove spikes with a sledgehammer to secure the rails to the ties; hard work with very low pay. While working for a local butcher, he was told to keep his finger on the scale when weighing meat so it could be sold for more than it was worth. He quit!

While working on a farm, he was kicked by a mule and suffered a broken leg. The farmer fired him because he couldn't work and gave him no pay. At the time my mom was pregnant with me. The most amazing fact is that he gave all his paychecks to his father until he was twenty-one! His father gave him an allowance and enough money to buy a car.

When he turned twenty-one, he was "allowed" to move out on his own. Can you imagine anything like that happening today? Today, it is common for "children" to go to school until they are well into their twenty's with the parents borrowing money to keep them in school. Quite a turn of events. Between his twenty-first birthday and his marriage when he was twenty-four years of age, he worked several jobs. He worked for the Gutwein Elevator & Grain Company in Francesville as a laborer. He also worked in a service station in Valparaiso. The station was owned by Ray Heinold who was my mom's cousin.

Mom also quit school when she turned sixteen. She did a variety of domestic jobs and for a while lived in Hollywood California with her older sisters, Alice and Clara. They were employees of John Barrymore, the famous Shakespearian actor, composer and writer. While today people may know the name Drew Barrymore, John will be unknown to most. Drew is his granddaughter. He had a magnificent home in Hollywood and the Heiniger sisters worked there for some time as cooks and maids.

My mom also worked later in Valparaiso with her sisters for the Lowenstein family in the same role. Mr. Lowenstein was the owner of a large steel and wire company in Chicago. The Lowenstein house was clearly the grandest home in Valparaiso. It was built in the 1920's and ironically it was owned later by my cousin Keith Heinold who was the third owner. As kids, our parents took us there to trick or treat as Aunt Clara was the one handing out the goodies.

Farming in the early part of the twentieth century was done primarily with horses and mules. My grandpa farmed with two teams of horses and two mules. In February of 1938 a major change occurred as he purchased his first tractor. It was an Allis Chalmers model WC. It had to be a bittersweet day for grandpa. The tractor would modernize his farm allowing them to get the field work done in a timely manner, but he loved his horses and that was surely a hard thing to see them leave the farm. Uncle Merle told me that he did keep one team of horses when he bought the tractor and for a few years both tractor and horses did the hard work.

I have seen early ads for tractors that emphasized the fact that you only had to "feed" the tractor while it was actually working where horses had to be fed every day all year. At my Uncle Ken's farm auction in 2000, I bought the 1938 Allis Chalmers. Some later research showed it to be a 1937 model. It was in very sad shape and had been parked since around 1960. When I was a teenager I drove this tractor on several occasions when helping bale hay at my grandpa's farm.

In the early 1950's my uncle Vernon's spring crops were totally destroyed by flooding. A group of local farmers, relatives and church members all descended on their farm to replant the corn and beans. My tractor that day was the old Allis WC. It is in the process of being restored and will hopefully be "on the road" soon. While cleaning out some of my grandpa's papers, the original bill of sale for the tractor was found. It noted that the dealer took the two horses and two mules in trade, allowing him two hundred dollars for the four animals.

During a visit with my Uncle Les, he told me how proud he was to be able to drive that new tractor. He also told me that Grandpa did not allow his sons to operate it at full throttle, but required them to only run the engine at about one half the maximum speed. My guess is that when he was not around it went as fast as possible. My earliest memory is from the middle 1940's and I do not remember any farming being done in our area with horses. During the depression, almost all small farmers used horses and mules to work the land and by the late 1940's thousands of horses and mules were replaced with tractors.

As a father of eight sons, Bert had a lot of experience with boys. I once heard him say, "One boy is a whole boy, two boys is a half-a-boy and three boys is no-boy at all."

My mother's father was Andrew Heiniger. His ancestors came to the U.S. from Switzerland. He also came to Indiana from Illinois with several brothers for farmland that was affordable. He and his wife Magdalena had nine children. My Mother Esther was born in Kouts, Indiana on April 17, 1917. She had three brothers and five sisters. None of them survive.

Aunt Madelyn died recently in Lancaster, Pa. at age ninety-three. They settled on a farm south of Kouts, Indiana and also were dairy farmers. Grandpa had one glass eye, the result of a farm accident while working with barbed wire. He also had very swollen and sore ankles, the result of spraining his ankles repeatedly as a young man which caused him to walk very slowly. I inherited his bad ankles and passed them on to my son. Recently, my grandson Christian thanked me for his "bad ankles."

Andrew also lost his farm during the depression. My early recollection of him was that of a beaten down man. He was kind and soft spoken. He could fix most anything and was given the nickname of "Handy Andy" by one of my dad's brothers. They gave Grandma the nickname of "Leapin' Lena" as she was very energetic and always on the move.

After Grandpa Heiniger lost his farm, he was unable to recover financially. After he lost the farm he farmed for a few more years and then moved to Valparaiso in 1943. He and Grandma lived with my aunts Clara and Alice. He spent his last working days as a janitor and dishwasher at Valparaiso University. Aunt Clara and Alice both had jobs that took care of the expenses.

Grandpa passed away on March 29, 1957 at the age of seventy-seven. He died of "natural causes." I believe that he had cancer. When he died, I was a pallbearer at his funeral. The six pallbearers were the oldest grandsons of his sons and daughters.

As we were going down the stairs of the funeral home to go to the cemetery, my cousin Cort said, "Be careful guys or grandpa will get all shook up." At the time that was an Elvis Presley song that was number one on the top 50 charts. Needless to say, we all laughed out loud. When we got into the car to leave the cemetery after the funeral, my mom's first question to me was "what was so funny?" She was not too pleased with Cort's humor.

One of my fondest recollections of him is the day he came to our farm and brought me his old 12-gauge double barrel shotgun. It was very old and had the hammers on the outside. He said to me with a smile, "Let's go hunting." He was in bad physical shape at that point. I was very honored to get his shotgun. Unfortunately, it was stolen many years later when our home was burglarized.

Grandma Heiniger was amazing. She earned her nickname. After Grandpa died she moved alone to a small house in Valparaiso as her two daughters both moved out of town. Aunt Clara headed for Alabama as a missionary to one of the poorest areas in the entire United States. Aunt Alice went to Phoenix to work as a nurse. Grandma lived alone until her death on June 2, 1965. She was eighty-six years old. The summer before she died, I agreed to paint her little house. I worked on it after my job at Firestone. One night I arrived a little later than usual and she was up on a ladder painting. She told me that she wanted to get it done and assumed I wasn't going to show up that night. She was a very social person and loved to be around people. One of my favorite stories was when she asked a friend that was going to a funeral if she could go along. Turned out she did not even know the deceased or any of the relatives. It was just a social gathering for her. She was a great lady!

As previously mentioned, the Buchers and the Heinigers were members of a small denomination called the Apostolic Christian Church. This church began in the 1830's in Switzerland as part of the Anabaptist movement. Anabaptist means "baptized again", and referred to those who were baptized as infants who were re-baptized as adults in their new faith. Persecution of those who did not believe child baptism was adequate was what drove many from those areas to the U.S.A. Many who stayed were burned at the stake, starved to death, mutilated and drowned.

William Penn traveled up the Rhine River recruiting colonists to Pennsylvania with the promise of religious freedom. The first apostolic church in the USA was formed in Upstate New York in 1847. It primarily existed in rural farming communities in the Midwest. It is very conservative in its doctrine and worship style. To this day, the men and women sit on opposite sides of the sanctuary during worship services and there are no pianos or organs. Ministers do not attend seminary, and are selected by a vote of the congregation. Since they are not paid, the ministers all have secular occupations, and some of the largest churches have four or five ministers.

When we got our first TV in the early 50's, Dad was criticized by a number of the members of the church. TV was considered "worldly" and today a large number of the members of the Apostolic Church still do not have television in their homes. There are two worship services each Sunday with lunch served between the services. I am told that this was started because most of the members of the church were farmers. They did their morning chores, went to church until afternoon and then went home and did evening chores.

Most city churches met on Sunday morning and Sunday night but that would have been a hardship for the farmers, particularly when they went to church by horse and buggy. Most of the founders of the Apostolic Church in the U.S.A. were from Switzerland, Germany's Rhine valley and the Alsace region which is now part of France.

When the Buchers, Heinigers, Heinolds and several other families moved to Indiana from Illinois in the early 1900's, they needed a church building for worship. The Apostolic church in Cissna Park, Illinois was building a new church as they had outgrown their building. They gave their old church to the new Indiana congregation. It was dismantled and moved by horses and wagons and reassembled in LaCrosse, Indiana. It is still standing today and used by another denomination as the LaCrosse congregation built a new church during the 1960's.

CHAPTER 2

December 11, 1942

I WAS BORN ON DECEMBER 11, 1942. As I stated earlier, my father was working as a hired hand on a nearby farm and shortly before I was born he was kicked by a mule and suffered a broken leg. The farmer he was working for told him that he couldn't work there any more since he was on crutches. He was still on crutches and "out of work" when I came along. Mom and Dad were living in a tiny house on my grandpa's farm. Everyone in the family referred to it as the "little house." It had four small rooms and was probably no more than eight hundred square feet in total. I recall that several of my uncles used the little house as their first residence when they were newly married. It was a few hundred feet from the main farm house.

Soon after I was born, my dad joined my mother's cousin, Harold Heinold and they rented a farm several miles south of Kouts Indiana. In addition to being related, Harold was a close friend of my parents. He was single at the time. We had a great relationship until his death in 1998. He apparently was like a big brother or uncle to me during my first three years. He lived with us in the large farm house and bought me my first dog, a Springer Spaniel named Buttons. He was a fine man who later started several businesses and became very wealthy and influential. Unlike many men who are self-made and wealthy, he was a very kind and humble man.

In the 1950's farmers often had a difficult time selling their hogs when they were ready for market. He started Heinold Hog Markets. He farmed during the daytime hours, bought hogs from local farmers and then drove them to Chicago during the night. He purchased or started hog markets in a number of towns all over the Midwest and eventually was the largest purchaser of hogs from farmers in the entire United States. He also helped many young men purchase farms when they did not have the financial ability to do so on their own.

Harold had an uncommon trait that I often admired. While he was a very successful businessman and whenever he saw me he always wanted to know about me, what I was doing, how my career was going etc. He never talked about himself and I often had to work to get him to tell me anything about what he was up to. I have no recollection of the time on that farm but my parents told me several stories about our time there.

The farm house was located less than a hundred feet from State Highway 49, a busy road. The first story is my favorite. My love of anything with wheels and a motor apparently began before I was three years old. The farm pickup truck was a pre-war Ford. (That is pre-World War II for you young folks.) It was parked in front of the house facing the highway with the key in the ignition. Apparently, I got into the truck on my own, turned on the key and pushed the starter button. It started and headed for the highway. Since I could not push on the accelerator, it died on the incline just before reaching the road. That is where my mother found me.

My mother told me another story of me heading off toward the fields in search of my dad and Harold. It was in the springtime when the barnyard was very muddy. I got to the middle of the barnyard and got stuck in the mud, manure, and unable to move in any direction. My cries got her attention and my dad rescued me. The result of these escapades and others was a harness and a leash attached to the clothes line. I apparently was like a dog that could only go back and forth but could not get into any mischief or danger.

My first memory as a child was moving to the farm south of Valparaiso where I spent the rest of my childhood. I do not know what month we moved, but it was sometime during the spring of 1945. Dad had been farming with Harold Heinold for several years and decided to go out on his own. He had very little money but was confident he could succeed. My first recollection and it is a very small one, is a farm truck loaded with furniture in the driveway. The farm house which I believe was built in the 1920's was in very poor condition as were all of the buildings on the farm. The farm had been recently purchased by Dr. Paul Vietzke, a family physician in Valparaiso. Doctor Vietzke was a fine man, a good doctor and a good landlord.

The farm was made up of what had been two farms and it had a total of about three hundred and fifty acres. About sixty acres was woods or wetlands so the actual tillable portion was about two hundred ninety acres. Dad would find out soon enough that the land was also in bad shape, full of rocks and lacking the normal nutrients that would ensure good crops. The normal term for my father's arrangement with the doctor was that of a "tenant" farmer. The standard arrangement was that the landlord provided the land and buildings and the farmer provided the equipment and the labor. At the end of the year they split whatever income came from the crops, animals, dairy etc.

Dr. Vietzke understood that the farm needed work and told my dad that he was welcome to make improvements to the buildings and he would pay for the materials if Dad provided the labor. During the first few years we lived there, Doc built a new dairy barn and steel corn storage building.

WE HAD THE SOIL TESTED and added fertilizer and lime each year until the soil was capable of producing good crops. Each year during plowing and planting season we picked up hundreds of rocks and deposited them at the end of the fields. Dad spent a lot of time each winter remodeling the farm house. He added several rooms and improved it in many ways. One thing did not change. We had one bathroom. When all of my brothers and sisters were born, there were seven of us living there which was a problem at times. Later Dad added a shower but it was in an unheated room so it was only useable in the spring, summer and fall. Today the house is owned by a distant cousin. She and her husband have totally remodeled the house.

Life on a dairy farm after the war was challenging for the Bucher family. In addition to Holstein cows, we had pigs and chickens. I am not sure exactly when I was pressed into service, but at a very young age I was taught that "chores" were something that was required if you were a male member of the family. Gathering the eggs, feeding the chickens and other tasks like feeding calves and pigs became a daily task.

For some reason, I was never a morning person but my dad got me up and out each morning to help. Over the years we had a number of other critters on the farm. For several years we had sheep and geese present a few times. Dairy cows, pigs and chickens were our mainstay and those three income producing animals were part of our farm until my dad sold them off sometime in the 1960's. Dad loved his dairy cows and the "milk check" we received each month was an important part of our income. We normally had about twenty five cows and one bull. That meant we were milking sixteen to eighteen cows at all times. That task took about one hour each morning and one hour each evening. Dad normally started his day at about 6 A.M.

Milking the cows was only part of the equation. During the warm months the cows spent their day in the pasture consuming grass, clover and alfalfa. We fed them a small amount of grain and supplements (like vitamins) but most of their food was from the field. During the winter when the cows did not have fresh grass to eat we fed them hay and silage. That meant climbing to the top of one of our two 40 foot silos and pitching down the silage needed for the day.

Silage is corn that is chopped up in the summertime and blown up into the silo. It consisted of the entire stalk of corn as well as the ear. It fermented and had a strong smell but the cows loved it and it was very nutritious. The hay was in the mow above the barn and was put there the prior summer. Straw was baled each summer as well and used for bedding for the cows and calves. We put straw on the concrete floor so the cows and calves did not have to lie on bare concrete. Straw was the stalks that were left after wheat and oats were harvested.

Feeding calves, cleaning the barn, and other tasks made up the "chores" that we did each day. As I got older and capable of doing all the tasks, we often worked together and got the work done in less time. Around 8 AM we went into the house for breakfast, which almost always consisted of eggs, toast, bacon, and potatoes. In the evening, the milking process again began about 4:30 and finished at about 6:30 when we went in for Supper. Often the noon meal, which we called dinner, was the large meal of the day and supper was lighter.

Working on the farm all morning meant a big appetite at noon, and a large "dinner" took care of the needs until supper. Until I was about sixteen years old I was very involved in the process of doing the chores each day. By then my brother Ardie who is six years younger than me took over, as I began working at jobs off the farm. On Sunday, my dad normally did the chores in the morning and I did them in the evening. For him it was a seven day a week job, lasting twelve plus hours each day, but he loved it. During the hours between "chores", six days a week the farm work was done. It was somewhat relaxed in the winter time since there was no field work to be done, but machinery maintenance, fence mending and work on the farm buildings kept Dad busy.

He had a great habit of taking a nap each day after dinner. He would go into the dining room where we had a big console radio. He would turn on the radio, lie down on the rug and sleep for about thirty minutes. In the spring time or whenever there was field work to be done he would forgo this luxury, eat and get back to work. When time in the field was critical as in planting or harvest time, mom would prepare dinner and take it to the field. We took a short break to eat and then back to work.

LIFE ON THE FARM WAS a lot of work but we did have some time for fun. Again, I am not sure of the exact time but when I was six or seven years old a nice pony named Ginger arrived at the farm. Apparently one day I rode her to the farthest part of the farm, across the back road, which was probably close to half a mile. I dismounted to relieve myself but neglected to tie Ginger. She decided to head for home leaving me to walk. I guess the parents were somewhat concerned when she returned without me. It was a long walk home. Later when I grew too large to ride her, we got a horse named Belle.

Farm life was also full of opportunity for injury. Working on a farm at that time was one of the most dangerous occupations one could pursue. Again my memory is faint, but apparently when I was quite young I found myself in the barnyard and somehow got between a cow and her new born calf. Dairy cows are normally pretty docile, but like any mother with a baby, cows can show their anger when their offspring are threatened. This cow apparently thought I was going to harm her calf and she charged me with her head down and plowed me over. She continued to run forward and amazingly, she did not step on me. I am sure I was thoroughly frightened and careful not to get into that predicament again. We had several cows that did not like anyone behind them when they were being milked and they kicked with power. That usually only happened once.

When we moved to the Vietzke farm in 1945 my dad was twenty eight years old and had very little money. He bought a small used tractor (Case SC) and plow, and slowly but surely purchased other needed farm equipment. With only one tractor he would often have to go to the field during planting or harvest time after the evening chores and work until late at night. A few years later Dad purchased an old Oliver 70 as a second tractor. That allowed both of us to work in the fields at the same time.

I am not exactly sure of when I started driving a tractor and doing actual field work, but I believe I was about seven years old. Today I am sure that would be called child abuse. Actually, most farm families consisted of lots of children as they worked on the farm and provided much needed labor.

I loved tractors and I loved to drive them. During my time on the family farm, we had six or seven different tractors, all of them purchased used. As a young farm boy I longed for a new tractor and asked Dad why we always had to buy used equipment? One day he took me to a farm auction where he bought a piece of used farm equipment. The farmer had gone bankrupt and everything he owned was being auctioned. Dad told me that it was sad, but that particular farmer always had to buy the biggest, newest equipment available. When he had a bad year he was unable to make his payments and lost everything. He told me that we got great bargains by purchasing equipment that was in excellent shape, but at a fraction of the price of new. He always had good equipment and he kept it in excellent condition. No matter how late the field work ended, tractors and equipment always went into the shed. It was near the end of his farming years in 1964 that he purchased the only new tractor he ever owned, a John Deere 3010.

As stated before, Dad only had ten years of formal education, but he was a man who never stopped learning. Farming was a life of isolation and many days neither Mom nor Dad left the farm. Television had very limited programming and I don't remember either parent spending much time watching TV. I do remember Dad spending most of his leisure time reading. He spent a lot of time reading the Bible as well as a variety of other books. He also spent time in the evening doing the paper work necessary to properly manage the family business. He kept very detailed records on each of his cows, such as when they had their last calf, when they were due to be bred again etc. He never used an accountant, but did his own taxes. He also helped several other people prepare their tax returns.

Needless to say, Mom played a huge role in the family. While she was not inclined to work in the fields or with the animals, she cooked three meals a day and during hay and harvesting time provided dinner for a number of workers. Her garden was big, and she grew almost everything we ate. We produced our own beef, pork, milk, eggs, potatoes, sweet corn, and almost every other vegetable and fruit that would grow in Indiana. She worked in the garden, canned and froze food all summer long. Orange juice was not readily available, as it is today, and even if it had been available it was not in our budget.

We had a vineyard of concord grapes and mom canned dozens of jars of grape juice. It was as good as or better than the Welch's juice we buy today. Each year we butchered a steer and filled the freezer with beef. I recall when I was very young the butchering process took place in our front yard. The steer was killed and the butchering process took place as it hung from a tree. After that year we took the steer to a processing plant to be killed. They packaged the meat according to my mother's instructions and a few days later we went and picked up the meat.

One of the first meals we had each year when a steer was butchered was fresh liver. I have always enjoyed liver, especially if it is fresh. A pig was also butchered each year. My grandpa Heiniger was skilled at the butchering process and made excellent sausage. While money was sometimes short, we never wanted for food of any kind.

Friday night was go to town night, all the stores were open and we purchased the groceries for the week. Salt, sugar, cereal, jello, flour, and etc. were typically the products she bought. The milk truck came each day to pick up our milk and he brought us butter, cottage cheese, ice cream and any other dairy products we couldn't produce. We had a pasteurizer in the milk house and each morning we pasteurized a gallon of milk. It was whole milk which tasted normal then but today would be like drinking cream. Fresh eggs were gathered each day from the hen house.

Doc Vietzke had an orchard on the farm that was his hobby. In those days, doctors did not work on Wednesday afternoons, so he came to the farm every Wednesday and most weekends to work in his orchard. He planted over two hundred dwarf fruit trees of every variety available. He grew apples, pears, plums, nectarines, peaches and others that I cannot remember. He gave the entire crop away and told us to eat whatever we wanted so we always had great fruit.

Like most farm wives, mom was a terrific cook. She baked almost every day and pies were her specialty. Dinner and supper were served at the normal time each day and if you were not there for some reason you were on your own. The refrigerator was always full of good leftovers.

While the food was great, I was not fond of the process that it took to provide it. I remember vividly on many summer days mom asking Dad at the breakfast table if he needed me that day.

While I never bonded with the cows, I did enjoy working in the fields and doing almost anything related such as working on fence, machinery etc. I hated working in the garden. I always hoped Dad would say he needed me for the day but on many occasions he told her I was hers. That meant I would be on the wrong end of a hoe, rake or shovel, or on my knees pulling weeds. Shelling bushels of peas and lima beans was not my favorite way of passing time on a summer day,

One not so fond memory involved Doc Vietzke. I don't know what year but I was about six or seven when one day he came to work in his orchard he asked me to help him. I don't remember what the task was but I was riding in his trailer which was attached to his tractor and we were headed into the orchard when he jerked out the clutch and the tractor lurched forward. I was thrown out the back of the trailer and I hit my head on a rock which apparently resulted in a large cut.

In those days, doctors made house calls as needed so he had his medical kit in his Cadillac. He shaved my head, stitched me up and we went back to work. I wore my hair very short in those days and thought the scar was a badge of honor.

I believe I got my "sales" gene from my mom. My mom's mother Magdalena, (sometimes spelled Magdalene) was a Heinold and the Heinold family was special. I already mentioned Harold, and what a successful man he was. His brother Ray started Heinold Oil Company which was operating until recently when it was sold. He also started Heinold and Feller Firestone where I got my first job. Ori, Art and Kenny were the other Heinold brothers and they were all excellent salesmen. Maryann was the only girl and she was outgoing and was and still is loved by all who know her.

Although Mom only had a ninth grade education, she had business savvy. My first memory of her business skills involved Christmas cards.

She was a representative for several card companies. She would start in the early fall and call on the doctors, lawyers, dentists and other professional people in our town. She sold them cards for their business and personal use and most were engraved. She made a nice profit each year from that business. She sold cards for many years and had a number of regular customers who bought from her each year. After I was grown and out of the house, she became an AMWAY dealer. She was very successful at this venture also and had a number of dealers that she sponsored. We teased her a lot about her "Scamway" business, but she was loyal and committed. She often helped Dad by going after parts needed for repairs and doing other errands that allowed him to keep working.

Mom was nobody to mess with. I recall a time when I did something that was not acceptable to her. I don't remember exactly what I did but I took off running around the outside of the house. She chased me with a broom and when it became obvious that I could outrun her she told me to stop and take my medicine or it would be worse when she told Dad. I stopped!

Discipline was not something Dad was shy about either. While I think I and all of my siblings were pretty compliant kids, when we were out of line we could expect discipline. One vivid memory was at the table in our kitchen. My dad sat at the end of the table and I sat on his left. Sue, Ardie, Laurie and Tim sat in order of birth. I don't remember the year but I believe I was in my early teens when I apparently made a remark to my mom that was disrespectful. I didn't see it coming but my dad's left hand hit me in the head and I was instantly on the floor against the wall looking up! That was a lesson that I remembered, and a great learning tool for my brothers and sisters. Dad was not a tall man, but his years of working on the railroad and on the farm gave him a powerful physique.

As I stated previously, my parents were devout Christians and church was not an option on Sunday morning. From nine months before I was born, until I was out of high school I attended every Sunday. One year it rained a lot during planting season. Dad was behind schedule for planting and he decided that he needed to do some field work after church. He spent several hours in the field before it was time to do the chores. Near our house on the farm was a little cottage in the woods. Dr. Vietzke's mother in law, Mrs. Mary Maunder lived there alone. She was a widow who was probably about seventy five years old. The next day she knocked on our door and asked to talk to Dad. While I don't know exactly what she told him, the message was that she knew that he was a Christian man and that she was disappointed that he was working in the field on a Sunday. She commented that it wasn't good for people to see a Christian man working on a Sunday.

He was much convicted after that conversation and to my knowledge that was the last time my dad ever did field work on a Sunday.

Several years during the summer, I was allowed to spend a week at Grandpa Bucher's farm. At that point only my uncle Don and Ken were still living at home and they were doing the majority of the farming. It was a fun week as they were in their late teens and I was eight to ten years old. I helped with the chores and just "hung out" with them. We rarely had soft drinks at home, but there was always a case of long neck Pepsi's at grandpas. Since I was one of the oldest grandchildren, they were like big brothers to me. My nickname for many years was "Menace" and they were responsible for giving it to me.

My grandfather's farm was about fifteen miles away and on a number of occasions my dad's younger brothers came to our farm to help with field work, hay baling or filling the silo. My uncle Merle told me a story about the time he and three of his brothers were baling hay in one of our fields. In those days, the haymaking field crew consisted of four people. One drove the tractor, one loaded the bales from the baler onto the wagon, and two sat on seats on the baler. More modern balers automatically tied the twine on the bales, but at that time the two men that sat on the baler manually tied the wire that held the bales together. Apparently I was sent to the field in our old pre-war Chevy pickup with cold drinks for the men. He said that they were slowly moving across the field on the baler when they looked up and saw the old pickup coming directly toward them at a high rate of speed.

Since I was so little that I had to look through the steering wheel to see, they could not see me and they thought the truck was out of control with no driver. They all jumped off and headed for the fence nearby. He said that when they turned to watch the truck plow into the baler I slowed up, stopped, and exited the truck with a thermos.

Farming was one of the most dangerous jobs in the country and many farmers lost fingers, arms, etc. Tractors were top heavy and it was not uncommon for one to tip over. Early tractors like my grandfather's first Allis Chalmers did not have starters and had to be cranked by hand, which sometimes resulted in broken arms. My dad insisted on safe operation of machinery and for the most part I complied. God was looking over me as I am very sure that I often drove tractors faster than was prudent or necessary.

When a farmer was injured in a farm accident Dad often commented that carelessness was the cause. Near the end of his farming career, probably in the summer of 1966, he had a serious accident. He was operating a machine called a feed grinder. It ground up corn and other grain to create feed for our cows. It was operated by a belt that was connected to a tractor. Brother Tim was sitting on the tractor seat and Dad apparently started the tractor and the belt came off the pulley on the tractor. Rather than turn the tractor off and start over, he apparently tried to put the belt back on a moving pulley. He was thrown to the ground. He suffered head injuries and a broken left arm. I recall that he was very distressed that he had not taken care to work safely. He did make a total recovery but was "out of action" for some time. The following year he sold the cows.

Family was very important. Our Sunday routine often included a trip to my grandparent's home after church for some refreshments. A number of my aunts, uncles and cousins would often stop too. Grandma always brought out cheese, crackers and some sausage. As soon as we had something to eat it was time to play ball. There was usually an area in a field close to the farmhouse that was suitable for a game of baseball. One memory of visits to Grandpa's farm was the outhouse. The farmhouse had only one bathroom and that was reserved for the women and girls. Just outside the back door of the farmhouse was the outhouse. It was a three-holer, which allowed three men or boys to do their business simultaneously. There was no toilet paper but an old Sears's catalogue served that purpose.

When we got home on Sunday afternoon we usually had a large meal after the milking was done. This was typically fried chicken, mashed potatoes, and a number of other dishes. My job was to grab two chickens and remove their heads so mom could cook them. A stump and a corn knife (sort of like a machete) did the job. After you cut the head off a chicken, they can run for a number of feet until they stop. Sometimes my brother Ardie and I would have a contest to see whose chicken would go the farthest.

My grandparent's home was also the gathering place for the Bucher Christmas. The farm house was large, but it is hard to describe the packed house when the whole family was there. I would estimate that in the early days, forty to fifty people packed the place, food was abundant and after the meal we opened presents. What an event.

When Grandpa retired and they moved to a smaller house in town, the local high school became the venue for our Bucher Christmas. By then there were four generations as I and many of my cousins were now married with children. I don't know how many attended but it was probably close to one hundred. Food was prepared and served in the cafeteria and after the meal was served we all went into the gym. Basketball was played on one end of the gym and the other end was utilized by the smaller kids. I recall Grandpa sitting and watching all the activity and I asked him how it felt to be responsible for all the family gathered there. He just smiled.

Some of our last visits to Grandpa's house before he and Grandma went to live at a retirement home were interesting. He had a refrigerator in the garage and while the women worked or sat in the kitchen, grandpa invited the men to the garage for some libation. He would open the refrigerator and get a beer out for each man. He would then take a shot glass out and fill it with a shot of whiskey. We took turns filling and emptying the shot glass and then drank our beer. After the last person drank from the shot glass, he put it back into the refrigerator. I guess the alcohol killed the germs. On one of our last visits to their house before they went into the nursing home, he invited Diann to join us in the garage. That was quite an honor and the only time I saw a female take part in that tradition.

When they were in their late 80's, the decision was made to move them to the Apostolic Christian Retirement home in Francesville Indiana, about twenty miles from their home in LaCrosse. While they were still in good health considering their age, Grandma was very forgetful and their children were concerned for their safety. Shortly before going to the home, Grandma was in church one Sunday and she met Ben Hitz, a man that she had known all of her life. She was having trouble remembering names and Ben asked her "Marie, do you know who I am?" Her answer was "do you know who you are?" When he said yes she said "that's all that counts" and walked away! She had a great sense of humor!

The retirement home was new and very nice, but they did not enjoy leaving their cozy little house and moving to a small apartment. On my first visit there I asked Grandpa how he was doing and his response was, "They've got me in a pen." For a while he had his big Chrysler there so he could head to town when he wanted, but when he was observed driving on the sidewalk the decision was made to take his keys. That also created another problem.

Grandpa liked a little nip of schnapps each night and the home was a "no alcohol" facility. Somehow he sweet talked some of the employees (female type) to bring him his supply. I forgot to mention that the manager of the facility was Grandpa's son, my uncle Elmer. I know Uncle Elmer had some challenges with his parents there, especially Grandpa.

When Grandpa turned ninety, I asked him how it felt. "Beats the alternative" he said with a smile. Grandma passed away on July 30, 1983 several years after arriving at the home. She was ninety years old. Grandpa lived another year and died on August 30, 1984 at age ninety two. They had a rich, full life together. They celebrated their seventieth anniversary and saw their twelve children all grow up and have families. Every one of their children and all of their spouses were Christians. One of Grandma's favorite sayings when they went through their many tough times was "the Lord will provide." He did and they left a great legacy.

While I do not know the exact year, sometime in the early 1950's Mom and Dad decided to take the family on an extended trip. That was a huge decision for a dairy farmer who took pride in taking care of his herd on a daily basis. He hired a young man who was our closest neighbor by the name of Phil Miller to take care of the farm. The trip was taken in the winter time, I think it was over Christmas break so there was no work needed on the farm except taking care of the animals. Phil was probably in his late teens at the time. Mom, Dad, Sue, Ardie and I piled in the 1951 Pontiac and headed for California. I do not remember how long we were gone, but it was at least two weeks.

We headed west in a somewhat middle route and returned via Phoenix and Texas. We spent time with my parent's friends, the Kinsingers in the L.A. area. While we were in L.A., Dad was following another vehicle too closely and when the driver in front hit the brakes, Dad did not and we plowed into him. The front of the Pontiac was crushed and it took a few extra days in town to get it fixed.

We then headed to Phoenix to visit Mom's sister Alice, and while we were there we experienced a rare ice storm. On to Texas for a visit with Lynn and Maryann Feller, who were stationed at Fort Sam Houston, and then back to Indiana.

A few other memories from this trip; One, was the motel choices. There were no chain motels so when we were tired of traveling, Dad would pick a motel and we would wait in the car while the attendant showed him a room. If he approved we piled out and if he did not, we moved on to another motel.

Some nights it took him two or three rejections until he approved of a unit. Chain restaurants were almost non-existent except for an occasional Howard Johnsons so almost all of our meals were at local diners. I was told that I ordered a burger, fries, and a chocolate milk shake at every stop.

When we got back to the farm we found all was well with one exception. When Phil went into one of the farm buildings to take care of animals, an owl attacked him and destroyed one of his eyes! Can you imagine the law suits that would result if that happened today. I have no idea what the financial results were, but I think Dad paid for this medical bills and that was the end of it.

CHAPTER 3

School Days - Grade 1- 8 1948 to 1956.

In September of 1947, I started first grade at the age of five. Almost all of my classmates were six years old except me and my friend and neighbor, Larry Lansing. We both were five years old and our birthdays were in December. Our parents were told that we could start early as a trial and if we could not keep up we would have to wait until the following year to start the first grade. Apparently we did okay as we were both allowed to stay. Morgan Township School was a rural two story school with a work shop building behind it. Morgan Township was almost entirely made up of farms except for a few homes in a very small town called Malden.

All twelve grades were in the same building with about two hundred students total. The lower level consisted of the cafeteria, gymnasium and boiler room. The first floor consisted of classrooms for grades one through six. Junior High and High School were on the top floor, along with the Principal's office. When I was in the seventh grade a new gymnasium and music room was built close by the old building. That was a big deal as our old Gym was very small and antiquated. My class consisted of about 18 kids in the first grade. There was no kindergarten.

My first grade teacher was Mrs. Aigner, a kind elderly lady. I don't recall a lot about my first few years of school, but I did enjoy it for the most part. School was easy and like most of the boys in my class, I did enough to get by. My grades were always good and elementary school did not require any homework. I did have a few issues in a subject called Deportment.

A reoccurring issue on my report cards seemed to be my verbal skills. "Talks too much" was mentioned by several of my teachers. I do not remember what my crime was, but do recall my fourth grade teacher, Mrs. Carlson sending me to see the principal, Mr. Howser. That meant two things were going to happen. Mr. Howser had a paddle and I would be the recipient of it and the word would get to my dad who would give me a second dose.

There was a boy's bathroom just outside the fourth grade room. When she sent me to see Mr. Howser, I went into the bathroom and stayed there for about ten or fifteen minutes. I then went back to my class and she never caught on! I guess she should have checked to see if I made it to the destination, but I was very happy that she didn't.

You could tell which kids lived on a hog farm as they brought some of the odor to school with them. I never went to school without taking a bath or shower after doing the morning chores. I rode the school bus from first grade until I got my driver's license in the middle of my junior year. The bus picked me up at the end of our lane and went directly to school, which was about two miles. After school I was the first student dropped off. Some kids had to ride the bus for an hour each way but living close to the school did have its advantages. The vast majority of the kids at Morgan were farm kids and most of our families were poor, but we didn't know it since we were all pretty much in the same boat. Our parents had vivid memories of the great depression, and in 1948 when I started school, World War II was a fresh memory. Each August my mother bought me two new pairs of blue jeans and two shirts, which was the wardrobe for the year. When looking at my class pictures recently, I noticed that I wore the same shirt in my first grade and third grade class picture.

Music was required during our first eight years of school. I enjoyed music and I sang in the school choir and enjoyed it. During those years, my Grandpa Bucher taught our Sunday school class how to read music. He was a gifted singer and led the singing at our church. He also was on the cutting edge of technology. I recall that he had a wire recorder, the predecessor of the tape recorder. He loved to record singing which was a major pastime. He then got a reel to reel tape recorder. He also had a machine that made recordings on records. I still have one of the records he made of me singing when I was four years old.

Just like today, we occasionally went on class trips. While schools today go to fun places like fire departments and museums, I recall a class trip that would probably not go over too well today. One morning after arriving at school, we boarded a bus and headed for Chicago which was about a two hour trip at the time. Our class trip was to the Chicago Stock Yards on the south side of the city. There, thousands of hogs and steers were received each day from farms all over the Midwest and slaughtered. Swift & Company and Armour Star Company both had large slaughter houses and packing plants near the stockyards. The animals were moved from the pens when they arrived by truck and processed. We spent the day on a tour of these plants and watched the entire process from the killing of the animals to the packaging of the product. Since we were almost all farm kids, this was fascinating as well as educational. After the morning tour we had lunch at the restaurant located in the same building as the processing plant. I still remember the great tasting cheeseburgers.

Being a rural school, all of the boys were required to take Shop class starting in the seventh grade. We learned wood working, machinery repair as well as a comprehensive study of agriculture and everything related to it. Mr. Ewalt was our Shop and Agriculture teacher and each day we ventured out to the shop building behind the school for one of his classes. I always enjoyed his classes and learned a lot about how to grow things and fix things from him. Learning to weld was one of my favorite things that he taught us. All the boys were required to join the Future Farmers of America (FFA) and most of us had 4-H projects that we exhibited at the county fair. One year the High School boys were given an old 1930's tractor and we restored it and then sold it.

The county fair was the highlight of the summer. It was always in the early part of August and it was great fun. There were always a lot of animals exhibited, rides and games on the midway, and great hamburgers, milk shakes and other assorted junk food. That may not sound like a big deal, but in those days we would eat almost every meal at home or at the home of a relative. Restaurants were rarely visited and "fast food" had not been invented, so the food at the county fair was a real treat. All of the car dealers exhibited the newest models and the farm equipment dealers brought the latest tractors and farm equipment. Each day there was animal judging. One day, it was pigs, the next dairy cows and calves, and beef cattle another day. Sheep, chickens, ducks and geese were also judged. Many of the girls brought homemaking projects and they were judged also.

Every night there was some kind of show at the grandstand. Joey Chitwood was a stunt driver and he brought his show several years. Cars jumping over other cars and crashing into each other was terrific fun for a kid to watch. Horse races and a variety of other shows including some well known musicians and comedians performed each year.

SINCE I HAD PIGS AT the fair for a number of years, I had to be there each day several times to feed them, clean the pens etc. I wasn't old enough to drive so I was allowed to spend several nights at my Grandma Heiniger's house which was only a few blocks from the fairgrounds. That was a big deal! Living on the farm with the closest friend a mile away could be a lonely existence for a young man, particularly one that loved to be around other kids. Fair week was by far the most fun week of the year for me.

I did not realize it at the time but my dad was preparing me for life during my years on the farm. Obviously, I did not become a farmer, but growing up on a farm prepared me for life and a career. As I stated before, my dad was a sharp businessman and a hard worker. He taught me that there was no free lunch and that hard work and excellence produces good results. He taught me that chores had to be done each day.

When I expressed a desire to enter pigs at the 4-H fair he told me that I could buy baby pigs, pay for the feed, and then keep the money I got when I sold them at the end of the fair. Several years he helped me purchase baby pigs from other growers. One year I won the best pen of three pigs and got the reserve (second place) grand champion. As I recall there were several hundred pigs exhibited so that was a big deal. When it came time to sell them at the auction, I got four times the going price per pound so I made quite a bit of money. Some years I won nothing and sold the pigs for little more than I had invested. It was a good way to learn how commerce works.

Dad had a number of sayings that may or may not have been original, but were certainly wise. He told me "I can't make you like to work, but I can teach you how to work." He also reminded me regularly that "anything worth doing is worth doing well." Once when he was referring to a fellow that he wasn't particularly fond of he said, "I would like to buy him for what he is worth and sell him for what he thinks he is worth." He told me to believe "half of what you see and none of what you hear" and I would not get in trouble. On several occasions, he reminded me to "never say never." He reminded me that whatever I did I should "do it for the Glory of God." He always encouraged me to try things that I had never done before. I recall one winter when I was a young teen he told me to take a tractor motor apart as the motor needed a minor overhaul. I told him I did not have a clue as to how to do that and he told me to get the tools and start. I got it apart and eventually got it back together and it ran! I am sure he assisted in the re-assembly, but he always encouraged me to "give it a try".

Dad was a humble man but as I look back, there is no doubt that he tried to do everything with excellence. A great example is the planting story. Our farm was along Indiana State highway 49 and that was the road that all his friends and relatives traveled when they went to town. I am not sure of the year, but he decided it was time for me to learn to plant corn. I was allowed to plant in a field near the back of the farm as he wanted to plant the field along the road. The reason - he wanted to be sure the rows were straight so they looked good to the many travelers that drove along highway 49 every day.

When soybeans were planted along the highway, we walked up and down every row chopping out any weeds or corn that was growing among the beans. Again, that was primarily for aesthetics. (The Bucher boys, and girls, including his grandkids and even great grandkids) are some of the most competitive people I know. Whether on the golf course, basketball court or a game of corn hole, winning seems to be very important. Again, looking back I see that Dad was competitive also. One year we had an unusual amount of rain in the spring delaying the planting of corn. Planting corn in wet ground is a bad idea that will yield bad results.

Dad always liked to be first to get his crops planted and first to get his crops harvested. That year, we were doing some work around the barnyard when he heard a tractor in a neighbor's field. We got into the pickup and headed out to see who was in the field. I don't remember the results of the investigation, but I do know that he was a man who liked to be first—do it right and most of all, do what was pleasing to God.

A major event happened when I was in Junior High School. Dr. Vietzke bought the farm in 1945 as an investment and a hobby. As I stated previously, he spent every Wednesday afternoon and many Saturdays and Sundays at the farm working in his orchard. He was constantly planting new fruit trees, and keeping up with the spraying, mowing, pruning, and fertilizing became more than a hobby, but he felt he was spending all his leisure time at the farm.

His hobby had turned into work. One day in 1955 or 1956, he came to see Dad. His message was simple. "Art, I have decided to sell the farm and before I advertise it, I want you to have the chance to buy it. Dad was very upset, as he was happy with his arrangement with a great landlord. Since both his grandfather and my mom's father lost their farms to foreclosure during the depression, he was very nervous about buying the farm. Moving and looking for another farm was also a very nerve-wracking prospect.

After much thought and prayer, he approached Harold Heinold, Mom's cousin and Dad's earlier business partner. Harold agreed to become a partner with Dad and they moved ahead and bought the farm together. Harold was an investor and did not get involved with the day to day operations, much like Doc Vietzke. As it turned out, Dad paid off his mortgage within a few years, and Harold was his partner until his death. Later, my siblings and I sold some land Dad owned in La Porte County and purchased Harold's portion of the farm.

Junior High School was the beginning of my sports career. We had Jr. High baseball and basketball teams that competed against the other schools in our area. I loved sports and was excited to be part of a real team. Dad helped me put a basket up in the second floor hay mow of our barn and I spent many hours shooting baskets there. When we put hay into the barn, he tried to leave the area by the basket open so I and other kids could play. We were not allowed to use the school Gym unless it was an official practice so our barn often was the place games were played. I remember coming home with my dad one Sunday and finding several cars and trucks in our yard. A group of young men were playing in the barn. When we went to see who was there, none of them were familiar, but they heard that the barn was available to anyone who wanted to play there. I doubt that would happen today.

I also practiced baseball by throwing a ball against the barn wall, hundreds of times. Little League baseball began at Morgan when I was eleven and I got to play two years. My last year I made the All Star team and went to LaPorte, Indiana for an All Star tournament. I played shortstop and pitched. As I stated earlier, the church my parents belonged to was very conservative and discouraged participation in sports. As far as I can remember, Dad and Mom never came to see me play any games, baseball or basketball.

Dad did attend one of my basketball games my senior year; more on that later. Dad did not discourage or encourage me to play organized sports. He did tell me that ball practice or games did not mean I was released from my chore duties. I either had to do them before or after practice or games. Not fun when you are exhausted from a two hour practice. I also had to find a ride home from practice or games. Sometimes I could ride my bike, but most of the time I had to ask an older teammate or a teammate's parents to drop me off.

I have a great memory of my dad taking me to Chicago's Wrigley field to see the Cubs play my St. Louis Cardinals. I saw my hero, Stan Musial play which is one of my fondest memories. It was more than forty years later until I got to see my Cardinals in person again.

While I was living in Philadelphia sometime around 1990, I was invited to go to St. Louis to meet with a supplier of equipment used to align vehicles and install and balance tires, Hunter Equipment Co. At the end of the day, the VP of sales asked if I would like to go to a ball game. Of course I said, yes, and we headed for Busch Stadium. When we arrived at the ball park, the usher took us to our seats and we went down the aisle to the very front row just beside the dugout. The owner of Hunter Equipment Company, the company I was visiting also owned twenty five percent of the Cardinals. We sat in the front row of the owner's box.

Before the game, Ozzie Smith (if you don't know who he is, look it up) came over to the box and signed a baseball for me. It is in a prominent spot in my office beside my Stan Musial autographed ball. The next time I would get to see the Cardinals was in Dallas in 2011, in game five of the World Series. Unfortunately the Cardinals lost that game, but came back to win the Series in seven games.

As I stated in chapter two, from an early age I loved anything with motors and wheels. During my pre-teen years I became very fond of cars. Although my dad always looked for a bargain when it came to his farm equipment, he always had a nice automobile. The first car I remember was a gray 1951 Pontiac four door. I have only a vague recollection of that car. I do remember well when we got our new 1954 Pontiac Chieftain.

I was in the sixth grade when Dad brought it home, and I recall I liked it but wished he had bought a hard top instead of a four door. It was all white when he bought it but he quickly took it to a body shop and got the top painted bright red. I was only twelve at the time but remember how great it was to ride in that new Pontiac. That was about the time I got serious about saving money for a car. Living on a farm meant isolation for a kid and I looked forward to the time that I could drive. My dad said I could get a car as soon as I turned sixteen and got a license but would have to pay for it myself. I got very focused on earning and saving money. I saved money from my 4-H projects and from selling scrap iron I found on the farm. This was also the time when I subscribed to Motor Trend, the most popular auto magazine at the time. I got my first issue in January of 1955 when I was thirteen years old. Soon after, I wrote a letter to the editor asking him about the future of Pontiac. I told him that I heard a rumor the Pontiac brand was about to be discontinued because it was felt that it was too much like the Oldsmobile. He said "no way." Little did he know that I was a prophet! Both Pontiac and Oldsmobile are now history.

My hunch was right, but it was a bit premature—about fifty-five years premature. I still possess the Motor Trend issues from 1955 and 1956, and the owner's manual for the 1954 Pontiac.

About that time when Dad didn't have work for me to do, I started working for a neighbor, Mr. Lee Williamson. His farm was across the highway from our farm. Mr. Williamson was an elderly curmudgeon of a man who hired me to do field work as he was getting up in years and couldn't work in the field for long periods of time. He paid me one dollar per hour and I was thrilled to have the opportunity to work for him. He was a unique character. He had been a widower for years and his home was an incredible mess. He was a hoarder (we didn't know that term at that time) and his dining room and living room only had a path about two feet wide to go through the house. Both sides of the path were full of junk, newspapers, magazines and other assorted stuff. Compared to the neat clean home I lived in, I could hardly believe the way he lived. He offered to feed me, but I preferred to take my food with me.

He required me to use the lowest gear on his tractor, making the work last longer than necessary. I don't know why he insisted on that, for safety or because he wanted to preserve his equipment. I do remember it being somewhat painful to go as slow as he wanted me to go. I worked for him for a number of years and saved all the money he paid me. Slowly but surely my bank account was growing.

I got my second bicycle when I was in the seventh grade. It was the latest and greatest, an "English racer." It was maroon in color, had narrow tires, three speeds, and hand brakes. I loved that bike and it allowed me to have some freedom to leave the farm and visit my friends. I rode to Malden, the very small town which was about three miles from our farm, and got soda pop and candy from one of the two small general stores that were there at the time. Occasionally, my mom would let me ride to town, usually during fair week. I often rode to visit my friend and classmate, Larry Lansing.

Larry and I both lived on dairy farms and we shared a love for baseball and basketball. We played sports together from grade school through our senior year. He lived about a mile from me on a gravel road. I often rode to his house to play ball and the ride was a bit of an adventure. Between his house and mine was another farm owned by the Litinski family. They were nice folks but their dog was not. He was big and mean. I always prayed that he would not see me coming up the road because if he did, he took after me and chased me for quite a distance. He never caught me, but he sure got my heart pumping.

I never really enjoyed my time spent at Larry's house as I was always thinking about the ride home, and hoping the dog wouldn't see me. After I had the bike for a couple of years, I bought a gas motor from my cousin Glenn Pfeiffer. It mounted on the front of the bike and had a wheel that turned the front tire. I do not know how fast it allowed me to go, but it did move along at a pretty good clip.

It was my first motorized vehicle and I had a lot of fun with it. I spent a lot of my spare time on my bike. We set up cement blocks in our yard with long boards and did "ramp to ramp" jumps, sometimes as high as two feet. No helmet, quite a few crashes, and I am still alive and somewhat coherent.

DURING THE YEARS I spent in Elementary and Junior High School, our family grew. First, my sister Suzanne was born on July 23, 1946, followed by my brother Ardie in 1948. Ardie's birthday was interesting as it the same as our Dad's, August 29. While that bit of trivia is interesting, how it happened is the real story. Mom thought it would be neat if her baby could be born on Dad's birthday so she took some "home medication", quinine to bring on the baby. It worked as the baby came so quickly that she gave birth to my brother at home in her bed. Apparently the home remedy worked so quickly that she was unable to even start for the hospital.

Ardie was born early in the morning on August 29 so she got her wish. I recall Dad talking to me in the yard that morning and he asked me if I knew where babies came from. I reminded him that we lived on a farm so the process of breeding and birth were somewhat ho-hum and routine. That was the extent of my formal sex education. Next in line was Laurie, born on September 17, 1952 and Tim made number five on February 10, 1956. It was boy, girl, boy, girl, boy and we were each at least two years apart. I am not sure how they planned and accomplished that, but it sure looks like it was planned. While we had the typical sibling battles, we generally got along pretty well.

I stated earlier that Dad made a lot of improvements to our farm house. He modernized the entire first floor, closed in a porch and added a small "family" room. My parent's bedroom was on the first floor and there were two bedrooms on the second floor. The first floor was heated by two oil burning stoves, one in the kitchen and one in the dining room. The living room was closed off in the winter. There was no heat on the second floor. Indiana winters can be very cold so we only spent sleeping time in our rooms in the winter.

Sue and Laurie occupied the large front bedroom and the small back room was for me and Ardie. Tim was born when I was in the eighth grade, and he slept downstairs until I left for college. Dad cut a hole in the ceiling of their bedroom at some point to let some warm air come up into our room. It did very little good, and I remember water in a glass freezing in our room when we had some very cold nights. Summers were no fun either as ninety-plus degree days were common. The only air conditioning we had was a big noisy window fan in the attic which was at the far end of the upstairs. Sometime during the early 50's Dad had a propane gas furnace installed in the basement. What a major improvement. Unfortunately, only one register was installed upstairs and it was in the hall between the bedrooms. Not much help.

CHAPTER 4

High School

To this day, I consider High School some of the best years of my life. I started my freshman year in the fall of 1955 as a thirteen year old. One of the first things I remember from the fall of my freshman year was a tradition called initiation. While initiation or hazing has made the news at many colleges and universities, often with tragic results, the initiation at Morgan Township High School was pretty tame by comparison. It started with all the freshmen boys dressing as females for the school day. We returned to school that night for the "fun." We had to participate in a number of activities, some a bit scary and some just fun. One that I remember was being required to take a Baby Ruth candy bar out of a toilet and eat it. I hope the toilet was cleaned before the process, but I am not sure. I doubt that initiation takes place at schools today.

Another activity that took place at Morgan was the "Slave Auction." We were always looking for ways to raise money for trips and projects and the slave auction was one of our fundraisers. Many farmers and homeowners came to the auction to "buy" a boy for a day. Each "slave" was brought out onto the stage at the end of the Gym in chains by two of the biggest boys in the school. All of the boys in the high school were auctioned to the highest bidder. We were required to show up and work for eight hours for the buyer. The older boys brought a bigger price than the young ones as they could do more work. I remember being purchased one year by a neighbor, Mr. Neil Ailes, and I spent the day doing a variety of jobs in his big yard. It was a fun event and we raised a lot of money, but I suspect Al Sharpton and Jesse Jackson would be in town the next day if any school tried this activity today.

Another fun time at school was the annual pest contest. This was an FFA activity that benefited the local farmers.

The boys were divided into two teams, with the goal of eliminating as many pests from the local farms as possible. Rodents and birds were costly to farmers as they consumed grain and spread disease. Rats, mice, pigeons, starlings and sparrows were the pests. For a period of a month, we "eliminated" as many of these critters as possible. This was done at night, and the following morning we brought the evidence to Mr. Awalt, our FFA advisor. We brought the heads of the birds and the tails of the rodents and he counted them and kept the tally. It was great fun.

The process of raising chickens at the time was to put baby chicks into a clean chicken house. By the time they were grown and ready to sell, a chicken house had a substantial amount of manure on the floor, often six inches or more. One night my team went to a farm with a chicken house that had just been emptied. We used flashlights and with pitchforks started digging in the manure. We hit the jackpot! Rats everywhere. Some of us dug and the rest used clubs to kill the rats. As I recall, we proudly took a large bag full of over one hundred rat tails to the school the next morning.

One night we went to a farm with a big barn that was full of pigeons. They were roosting on the rail at the top of the barn, some thirty feet or more above the floor. One of the older boys on the team climbed to the top of the barn and slowly made his way across the barn pulling the heads off the birds as he went. That was a big haul and again, the next morning was a time of celebration as we turned in a large quantity of heads.

In addition to the team outings, we all worked to eliminate any pests from our own farms as possible. My BB gun and my .22 rifle were in constant use on the farm and I wiped out as many birds as possible. I imagine that there were some incidents on school busses as the boys took the heads and tails to school each morning. The competition between teams was fierce and the winning team was served dinner by the losers.

As I recall, I was on the winning team two years and the losing team two years.

Every other year there was a class trip for the Junior and Senior classes. As soon as we started our freshman year, we began the process of earning and saving money to go on the trip. Bake sales, scrap drives and many other fundraisers were constantly going on for our first three years of high school. By the time we left for our trip in the spring of our junior year, we had saved enough money so that every kid could go.

There were about forty kids in the two classes and we went on a trip to New York City and Washington D.C. Four teachers accompanied us as chaperones and advisors and it was an amazing adventure for sixteen, seventeen, and eighteen year old kids. We boarded a train in Valparaiso and went directly to New York. We toured the United Nations, the Empire State Building, and went to Radio City Music Hall. We saw the Rocketts and another show.

We stayed at the Henry Hudson Hotel, which is a twenty-seven story structure on W. 57th street. I was one of twelve boys who stayed in a four bedroom suite. No sleep! The first night after we were told to bed down for the night, we slipped out of the hotel and toured New York City on our own. Amazingly, no one got into trouble and no one got lost. Anyone who went to sleep got shaving cream in their mouth or other orifices so we pretty much didn't sleep. Indiana farm kids, many who had never been far from home were amazed by the Big Apple.

The subway, the automat, and just the constant activity night and day were a sharp contrast from our lives at home. After three days in New York, it was time to take the train to Washington, D.C. There we visited the Capitol, and saw the Senate and House of Representatives in session. We also visited the Supreme Court, Ford's Theatre, all the monuments, and the Bureau of Engraving and Printing where we saw money printed. Arlington National Cemetery and the Naval Academy rounded out the trip.

We were very busy for three more days and then headed home for Indiana. It was a memorable week and a great learning experience for all of us. We slept most of the way home, catching up on the sleep we didn't get while in the big cities.

Many years later on a business trip to New York, I made a point of visiting the Henry Hudson. Reflecting back, it wasn't exactly the finest hotel in 1959 and when I visited it in the 70's it was in bad shape and had been turned into a hotel with apartments for low income folks, and down, and outers. Definitely not a place one would want to stay. I imagine today it has been renovated and is now a good hotel again.

One of the fundraisers that occurred each year was the Jr. Sr. Class play. I had no particular interest in acting, but both years I was picked for the lead role. Our advisor, Mrs. Uban, selected plays by the same author both years and I played the same character, Wilbur Maxwell. One play was called the Boarding House Reach and the other was Finders Creepers. As I reflect back on those plays, I am sure they were not very good but they were very well attended. In our rural community, the school was the center of most activity. People who had no children or whose children were grown came to school events on a regular basis.

One good feature of a small school is the fact that every student has the opportunity to participate in a variety of extra-curricular activities. In addition to FFA, there was a school band, a choir, booster club, class plays and four boy's sports. In addition to basketball and baseball which were the two most popular sports, we had a track team and a cross country team. I played on the varsity baseball team all four years. My freshman and sophomore years were spent on the junior varsity basketball team, with my junior and senior years on the varsity.

While I was not particularly talented at any track or field event, I did have some success in the mile run. Cross country at the time was two miles, and Morgan fielded a team in that sport for the first time during my sophomore year. Coach John Starks was the coach of all four sports. He strongly encouraged all boys that wanted to play basketball to run cross country as it was held in the fall and would help get us into condition for basketball. Again, I was not particularly fast, but I did enjoy it and as it turned out I finished first for Morgan at almost every meet.

I stopped running after high school, but began again in my late twenty's and ran consistently until I was in my middle sixty's. I have been very blessed with good health all my life and I attribute that to two things. Picking the right parents and keeping in good physical shape.

Basketball was THE sport in Indiana. The movie 'Hoosiers' was a great example of how crazy the folks there are about the sport. While it was fiction, it was loosely based on the 1954 State Championship by a small school in central Indiana called Milan. Morgan Township had a very small population, but on Friday nights the gym was packed. It was the primary social event in the area and most of the residents attended the games, even if they had no kids. Almost every student in Junior High and High school attended the games as well. The Junior Varsity played first followed by the Varsity. Cheerleaders actually led cheers and the fans all participated. I lived for basketball. I spent most of my spare time shooting baskets and did that year round.

Terms have changed, but today I guess I would have been called a point guard. I typically brought the ball up the court and tried to be the quarterback of the team. My senior year I was the team Captain. We finished in the middle of the pack compared to the rest of the teams in our conference.

There are a few stories that I recall from my basketball career. The first one was from my freshman year. We were playing the Westville High School which was a school in the neighboring county. Unfortunately, Westville High did not have a gym that was acceptable for a high school game but the Westville State Mental Hospital which was nearby did have a great gym. We traveled to the hospital on the team bus, and we were told before we got there to stay together when going in and out of the gym. The J.V game was first. We showered and sat on the bench behind the team for the varsity game. I don't remember anything about the game but the audience was very interesting. The hospital had all levels of folks with mental disorders. Some had very mild cases and were no risk. They were allowed into the gym to watch the game. Some were dangerous and of course they were confined to their cells or rooms.

During the game a number of strange things happened. One fellow spent the entire game switching his socks from his left foot to his right and then back again. Two other guys got into a fight and had to be removed. We youngsters were wide-eyed and a bit nervous during the game. After the game, we all went to the locker room and waited for the varsity to shower so we could go to the bus as a group. One member of the varsity team was a senior named Ron Kastner. Ron was very nervous about going to a mental hospital and made several comments about his fears on the way to the game.

Unfortunately after the game, he was so nervous that he didn't pay attention to the instructions and got separated from the group. When the bus was ready to leave, someone noticed that Ron was not on board. The coach went back and after a bit of searching for him located Ron. He was scared to death. He apparently told a security guard that he didn't belong there and the guard said "that's what they all say." We all had a good laugh but Ron didn't think it was funny.

During my junior year we had a young team with four juniors and one senior on the starting five. We won a number of games, but did not have a winning season. At the time, all teams in Indiana competed in the same state tournament, regardless of the size of the school. The first level was called the Sectional and included twelve local teams, and the teams were paired up by a drawing. We were unfortunate enough to draw Valparaiso High School. In 1959, Valpo was ranked as high as number one in the state. Four of the starters were seniors.

WHAT IS ALMOST UNBELIEVABLE is that all the starting five in 1959 went to Division 1 colleges on scholarship. It was a very tough night. We lost ninety three to thirty four. They were big, fast and very talented and definitely out of our league. A neat fact is that one of the guards from that team was Scotty Ward. He went on to star at South Carolina University and is in the SCU hall of fame. He is a legend in Valparaiso and was an amazing shooter.

Every August, I join a bunch of guys who grew up in Valpo for four days of golf and Scotty is one of the group. He was out of my league in basketball, but he has yet to beat me on the golf course.

After every home basketball game, tradition and hunger caused us to head to town for some food. One night, I was riding "shotgun" with Larry Lansing when we stopped at highway US 30. It is a four lane road with lots of traffic traveling at high speed. While we were waiting for traffic to clear, we were rear ended by a fellow student, Glen Tyson. He had no driver's license and had taken his Dad's car without permission and ran into us going about thirty to forty miles per hour. Larry's car, a '57 Ford, was driven across the four lanes, the front seat was ripped loose and was against the back seat. It was a total loss. Other than stiff necks, we amazingly were uninjured. It is incredible that we crossed four lanes, and were not hit by oncoming traffic. God was surely watching over us.

Another basketball story took place during my senior year. The closest school to ours was in the town of Kouts. It was a much bigger school than ours and was our biggest rival. We lost our first game to them in their gym early in the season. The last game of the season and the last home game of my career was against Kouts in our gym. As I stated earlier, my dad did not attend any of my athletic events. I was often asked why he never attended and I really did not have a good answer.

I suppose it bothered me when I was younger but after a few years I really did not think about it. The final game against Kouts was one of the best games I ever played. Several things made it special. We won the game and that was a great way to end the season. Most special was the fact that my dad came to the game. My dad's two youngest brothers, Don and Ken went to our house and told Dad to get ready because they were taking him to the game. Seeing my dad and uncles in the bleachers was a great way to end my high school basketball career.

Some of our basketball practices were held in the evening which meant Mom or Dad had to take me back to school or I had to bum a ride with an older teammate. During my junior year before I got my license my dad allowed me to drive our old pickup to practice as long as I went only on the back gravel roads. In total, the one point five mile trip took about four miles, but Dad allowed it as there was very little traffic on the gravel roads and very little chance of a problem. I had been driving the truck on the farm for a number of years so I was very competent, or so I thought. On the way to practice I stopped to pick up Marvin King who was a year younger than I was.

At an alumnae event a few years ago he reminded me that after picking him up I always stopped on a wooden bridge near his house, pushed the gas pedal to the floor and popped the clutch. That tired old truck would spin its tires on the wooden bridge and smoke would roll.

What fun! Thank goodness Dad never found out about that. Imagine today a fifteen year old kid allowed to drive to school, with no driver's license and pick up another kid on the way; very unlikely.

Baseball was my second favorite sport. We played baseball anytime we had spare time and there was enough daylight to see. We played at recess, lunch time and any other time weather would permit. We played any time we had four or five kids and most farms had an area where we could play. In the 1950's, there were only three TV stations, no electronic games and unless it was dark, we were outside doing something physical, usually involving a ball. As a freshman, I made the varsity baseball team. I was very small and played very little. The only game I can remember was a game played at Liberty Township School. It was the seventh inning and the game was tied. The sun was setting and it was getting a bit hard to see. With the bases loaded, Coach Studer put me in as a pinch hitter.

Ever since I was a little kid, my hero was Stan Musial, the hall of fame player for the St. Louis Cardinals. He had a unique batting stance that made the strike zone somewhat smaller. It was described as a crouch. From my youngest days of swinging a bat, I tried to emulate his stance. On that October day, coach told me to get up to bat, get into my crouch and try to get a walk. It worked! The pitcher couldn't get the ball down into the small strike zone and he threw four straight balls. I walked and the winning run came in.

During the next three years I played regularly as a shortstop, second baseman, and occasionally I pitched. I loved to play baseball. When my son David played little league I was an assistant coach and after I retired to New Bern I coached little league for several years. I was fortunate to coach my Grandson Christian one year.

I turned sixteen in December 1958, my junior year. That marked the beginning of a lot of changes in my life. I had completed driver's education at school during my sophomore year so I went for my license the day after my birthday and passed with flying colors. As promised,

Dad allowed me to buy my first car. It was a 1956 Chevy Bel Air two door hardtop, black and white with a black and silver interior. It had a V-8 engine and was the sharpest car in the Morgan Township School parking lot, including the teacher's cars. I am sure that it did not hurt my future dating activities as most kids either, drove their Dad's car, or some type of junker. Since I had saved my money for a number of years I was able to pay cash for the car. One thousand and one hundred dollars!

TO PAY CASH FOR A TWO year old car was quite an accomplishment. In 1958 the average full time blue collar job paid about four thousand to five thousand dollars annually so one thousand and one hundred dollars was a lot of money. Since I still was responsible for chores and worked in the fields as needed, Dad allowed me to take ten gallons of gas from the farm gas tank each week. I am sure that occasionally I took a bit more and I am sure Dad knew that, but he never said anything. That car was my pride and joy. I washed and waxed it constantly and made a few modifications that made it one of a kind. Dual exhausts and steel pack mufflers gave it a great sound, and the removal of the hood ornament made it look sleek.

Sometime in the summer of 1959 the transmission of my Chevy broke. I do not know what caused the problem, but most likely it was abuse on my part. The result was a car that had no reverse and only high gear. I spent several months being very careful about where I parked. After I saved three hundred dollars, I had it rebuilt and it was as good as new. I recently saw a similar car on the internet advertised for sixty thousand dollars. How I wish I knew then what I know today.

My turning sixteen gave my dad some flexibility as well. While he loved being a dairy farmer, it was a very demanding existence. While he has some free time between 9 AM and 5 PM, the cows were always waiting to be milked. Since I now could drive and take care of myself, sometime during the summer of 1959 my parents decided to take a vacation and leave me behind to take care of the farm. I don't recall how many days were involved but I believe it was five or six. Since it was after the crops were planted and before harvest time, very little work was needed to be done in the fields but the cows, pigs, chickens etc. had to be attended too.

One night I stayed out a bit late and for some reason my alarm did not wake me. I woke up after 10 AM! Needless to say I ran to the barn and got the cows in to be milked as fast as I could. Many of them were "leaking" milk from their teats as their udders were totally full. None of them suffered any permanent damage but I was sure worried for a while. One night during that week, the word got out that there was a party at Bucher's house. There were dozens of people going in and out of the house that night and some guys spent the night. While I knew most of the participants, there were a number of people that I did not know.

There was some damage done that night so I had no choice but to disclose the fact that a party had taken place. That was the first and last time that a party took place at my house.

SHORTLY AFTER MY SIXTEENTH birthday, I got my first real job. About a year earlier, my dad sold a building lot in the woods next to our house to his cousin, Lynn Feller. Lynn and his wife built a nice brick home. Lynn's wife was the former Mary Ann Heinold, my mother's cousin. Lynn had been a farmer in Illinois where he grew up, but he moved to Valpo to join his brother in law, Ray Heinold in business. Ray had sold tires from his oil bulk plant in the middle of town for several years, and in 1958 he acquired an empty car dealership building to start a retail tire store. Lynn came to Valpo to manage the new Heinold and Feller Firestone dealership.

Soon after I turned sixteen, Lynn offered me a part time job. I worked some days after school and most Saturdays. I loved working at the tire store. In the beginning my job was to do anything that no one else wanted to do. I mounted tires, installed batteries, installed seat covers, made deliveries and generally did whatever was needed. After a few months I was also doing service calls for both truck tires and farm tires. You haven't lived until you change a truck tire on the side of a busy road or fixed a flat on a tractor in a muddy field.

While the pay was not too great, it was a wonderful way to enter the work force and a great learning experience. Since I loved cars, the opportunity to work on them and get paid for it was a dream job. In the summer, I was able to work full time.

A guy by the name of Scott Newberry worked there with me that summer. He was a year older and was a crazy guy. One sunny day, Lynn gave Scott and me the task of putting pennants up in front of the store. My task was to climb a ladder to the roof and nail the end of the pennants to the roof. I then threw them to Scott who would attach the other end to a wire which ran from the corners of the building to a pole in front of the building, giving the effect of a canopy. We borrowed a ladder truck from Heinold Oil Company and I took a box of pennants up on the roof while Scott manned the truck. I tied a pennant to the front of the building and threw the pennant to Scott. He climbed the ladder and tied it to the wire that ran from the building to the pole. He had to move the truck for each pennant so the process took all morning. After we finished, Scott drove the truck away, but forgot to lower the ladder first. It made a tremendous noise and the wire and the pennants came crashing down. Both Scott and I lost it! I was still on the roof and Scott stood beside the truck doubled over in laughter. Lynn came out of the store with steam coming out of his ears. Later in my career I understood how he felt.

My cousin and good friend, Keith Heinold, worked across the street at one of his Dad's service stations. It was during my tenure at Heinold and Feller that my life's work would begin, but of course I had no idea at the time that would be the case. I also met one of my life-long friends while working there, A.B. (Bud) Wade who was the assistant manager at Heinold and Feller.

As every parent of a teenager is aware, obtaining a driver's license is a big change in the family dynamics. The teenager sees it as freedom, particularly when living in a rural area. To the parent it was good news and bad news. It reduced the number of trips the parent had to make to school events, but it increased the number of gray hairs caused by worry. Having a fast car necessitated proving it could beat other fast cars. That sport is called drag racing and it was done on a legal track and on the highway.

The highway that bordered our farm was newly paved concrete and was one of the more popular drag racing spots. Although I did not often participate in racing, my mother told me that she laid awake most nights listening to the squealing tires and the loud exhaust of the cars that raced on the highway, thinking that I was involved and worrying that there would be an accident.

I did gather in a few speeding tickets during my teen years. The price of a ticket at that time was one dollar plus costs, for a total of seventeen dollars and fifty cents. It doesn't sound like much, but when one's pay is one dollar per hour before tax, it was painful. One of my most memorable experiences with the law took place in La Crosse, Indiana which was the town where we attended church. On that occasion, my parents were out of town for the weekend, but the rule was "as long as you live here you will attend church."

I went to church that Sunday and after the morning service, I, and my friends, went to the local greasy spoon to eat lunch and play pin ball. On the trip back to church, my cousin Glenn Pfeiffer and I were driving a bit too fast for the liking of the local town Constable, Louie Lord. He pulled us both over and asked for my license. When he saw my last name he asked what relation I was to Bert Bucher. When I told him Bert was my Grandfather, he looked at his watch and said, "He must be going into church about now," and told me to follow him to the church. He marched into the sanctuary in full uniform and asked my Granddad to come out to the lobby.

Needless to say that was a big event! He told Granddad that I had been driving too fast through town, and then he turned and left. I sure wish he had given me a ticket instead. I don't remember the exact details, but needless to say my dad got an update from Granddad and my Chevy was in "time out" for a week or so. As I was relating that story to one of my cousins recently, he told me that Louie Lord was the Lacrosse version of Barney Fife of the Andy Griffith show.

Owning a car also meant freedom to date. Prior to my sixteenth birthday I had a few dates, but they were always double dates with an older friend. Having a car changed that. During my high school years I dated a few different girls both from my school and other schools around the county, but never had anyone that I would call a "girl-friend."

Morgan Township School was unique in a number of ways. It was very small. During the time I spent there, the total enrollment for grades one through twelve was approximately two hundred students. My class in high school had seventeen to twenty members with seventeen actually graduating. Mr. Don Guilford was the principal during most of my time there and he ran the school his way, which was very rigid. He would not allow anyone to drive an automobile to school unless they were a senior. Underclassmen could only drive to school if there were after school activities such as sports practice. Bicycles were not allowed to be ridden to school. Every student was required to eat their lunch in the cafeteria, and all students were required to purchase lunch from the school. No one could bring their lunch from home. No one could leave the school grounds at any time during the school day, even seniors who had cars. While we felt he was a dictator, our parents generally supported his rules.

When my mother died in 2000, Mr. Guilford came to the viewing. He was in his 80's and he walked with a cane but seemed very sharp mentally. He commented to me that he always respected my mom and dad and that they were always supportive of him. He celebrated his 100th birthday this year. (2017)

One day in my junior year I was summoned to Mr. Guilford's office. That usually meant trouble but on this day I was unaware of any deed that I had done that would warrant discipline. He wanted to cover two subjects with me. First, he wanted me to know that Coach Starks had gotten some "heat" from a member of the school board who had a son on the basketball team. This teammate was a senior and his father told the coach that his son was better than I and should be a starter on the team. Apparently Coach ignored this gentleman and did so at some risk. Mr. Guilford wanted me to know that Coach stood his ground.

I always admired and respected Coach Starks, but even more so after that meeting. The second subject had to do with my academic performance. Apparently we had just completed some testing. He told me that I had tested at the top of the class, but my grades were well below several other classmates. (All girls.) He wanted me to know that he felt that I was not living up to my potential, which no doubt was true. I always maintained a B or better average, but did very little in the way of studying or homework. He encouraged me to work harder at my studies and to prepare for college. I admit that until that meeting I had given little thought to what I wanted to do with my life. I am sure that being a principal in a rural farm community was frustrating as very few students went to college. Almost every kid in my class lived on a farm and most planned to be farmers or do other blue collar jobs. Graduation from High School in 1960 was good enough for most jobs, and the dropout rate was quite high.

Another time I was invited to visit with Mr. Guilford occurred in my senior year. One evening after basketball practice, I, and three of my teammates, went to town to have some pizza. On the way home as we were passing my dad's farm, someone noticed a large sign at the end of our farm advertising Larry's Drive In. It was about six feet wide, four or five feet tall and it had a large metal Pepsi Bottle cap attached to it. The cap was about two feet across. Two four by fours went several feet into the ground to support the sign. In it probably weighed several hundred pounds.

Someone came up with the idea of pulling it out of the ground and dragging it the mile or so to the school. Larry was a mean guy. His drive in was the only restaurant in our area and when we went there, he often refused to serve us for no good reason. He was surly to most customers. My dad went there one day and asked for a milk shake and Larry told him he didn't feel like making him one and he didn't. I remember commenting that the sign appeared to be on "my" property and he had no permission to put it there. So on that fateful night we pulled the sign out of the ground and two of us sat in the trunk and held on to the sign. The metal Pepsi cap was on the concrete road and sparks flew for about ten feet as we dragged it down the road. We leaned it up against the main door of the school and went home.

When I pulled into the school the next day, there was a State Police car and a Sheriff's car in the parking lot at school. Mr. Guilford had a pretty good idea who was involved and he called a number of boys into his office that morning, myself included. He asked me what I had done the prior night and I told him basketball practice, pizza and home. He got the same answer from all of us and even though he knew we were involved he couldn't prove it. After school that day we went to Larry's for some food. He refused to serve us and told us he knew we tore out his sign. We left and I don't recall ever going there again. I guess he never attended any seminars that teach customer satisfaction. What we did was wrong and repercussions could have been severe, but it sure was fun and seemed appropriate at the time.

After I graduated from high school, I needed to find work during the summer before I headed off to College. I wasn't needed full time at the tire store so I got a job working for Mr. Dwight Smoker, a farmer in the nearby town of Wanatah. Mr. Smoker had one of the largest farms in the area. Most of the crops he grew were to feed his large herd of Black Angus beef cattle. His son Jim worked the farm full time and he had a full time hired man year round.

For the summer of 1960, I was hired man number two. My schedule was simple. Start at 8 AM six days a week and work until at least 6 PM. We baled hay three or four days a week and my job was always the same. Load the bales as they came out of the baler onto the wagons. It seemed like the bales never stopped coming. On a good day we baled about a thousand bales. Jim drove the tractor that pulled the baler. Dwight drove the tractor that took the bales to the barn and the hired man unloaded them. Day after day this was the routine.

I remember being amazed and somewhat frustrated that Jim never offered to load bales and give me a break, not even for one load a day. Each day at dinner time the Smokers went into the house for a meal and I and the hired hand either brought our food from home or went into town for a burger. Traditionally, most farmers feed their workers at noon time but the Smokers apparently missed the class when that subject was taught. One dollar per hour translated to about sixty dollars a week. I sure was not sorry when summer ended and it was time to go to college.

CHAPTER 5

Indiana University

My two cousins, Wes Bucher and Nile Bucher also graduated in 1960 and we all headed off to college. I believe we were the first kids in our family to go beyond high school. Dad was somewhat cool toward the idea. He neither, encouraged or discouraged me. He told me that he would pay half of my room, board, tuition and books. I was responsible for the other half as well as spending money. Since I needed money and since freshmen could not have cars on campus, I reluctantly sold my 56 Chevy. I recall that tuition at state schools like I.U. at that time was somewhere in the range of a thousand dollars per year. That was big money at the time.

Dad used the same formula for all of my brothers and sisters. My sister Laurie did not choose to go to college so Dad gave her money to buy a car. She bought a sharp little Camaro. Wes and I went to I.U. and Nile headed for Purdue. I.U. is a huge university. Today, the I.U. enrollment is somewhere in the area of forty thousand students and in 1960 it was close to thirty thousand. Coming from a class of seventeen to a freshman class of about nine thousand was certainly a big adjustment. Wes, and I and our parents all made the three hour drive to Bloomington to begin our college days. All six of us were in one car, with our personal items, clothes etc. in the trunk. Our parents checked us into our room and headed home.

From the time we were little kids, we were best friends, so it was natural that we decided to be roommates. We lived in Wright Quadrangle, the largest all male dorm, with about nine hundred residents.

On a visit to IU recently, I saw that Wright Quad was still in use. As soon as I got settled in I got a job working in the cafeteria of a girl's dorm next to mine. I worked about fifteen to twenty hours a week which provided me with necessary spending money.

Attending classes with two hundred plus students was quite different from my high school experience. At seventeen years of age, I was not prepared for the discipline necessary for college. I did not have good study habits and my grades were a reflection of that. I did have a lot of great experiences that first year.

Every male student at I.U. was required to complete four semesters of ROTC. While it was not exactly fun, it was good training and would make life a lot easier when I went into Army basic training. I enjoyed my business courses and especially enjoyed my psychology class. It was three hours a week in class and two hours of rat lab. I had a great rat and during the semester it was amazing what he learned.

I only returned home four or five times during my freshman year, and each time I had to find a ride with someone who was headed toward Valpo. One trip was particularly memorable. I got a ride with a guy from my area and four of us headed home on a Friday night. It was a cold night with a freezing rain falling. My chauffeur did not feel the need to slow down and after rounding a bend, we slid sideways on the highway and began to roll over. The car did not have seat belts so we were all over the inside of the vehicle. I do not know how many times we rolled but it was several. We came to rest upside down in a deep ditch. A high school wrestling team coming the other way saw the accident. They helped us out of the car and amazingly none of us were injured. My coat was torn but that was the extent of my damage. As we were climbing out of the windows, gas was coming into the car.

Once again, God was looking after me. I did not ride with that guy again.

MY FRESHMAN YEAR WENT quickly and I was back home for the summer. After I left for school, my youngest brother Tim took my place in the boy's bedroom. From that time on whenever I was home on the farm, I slept in the attic. It was an unfinished room behind my sister's bedroom. The ascetics were bad, but it was roomy and private, which was all I cared about. The only downside was the large fan in the window that was our air conditioning. It sounded like an airplane about to take off. That was the summer of 1961, and the first thing I had to do was get some wheels.

A local used car dealership was owned by a man by the name of Truman Gaines. He was a good guy and I often stopped to chat with him. He sold me a 1955 Chevy for three hundred dollars. It was the very basic model with a six cylinder engine. It had some rust holes in the body, but mechanically it was in good shape. It was a big step down from my first car, but it was served the purpose as good transportation.

SOMETIME DURING THE summer, I did some bodywork to repair the rust and then took it to Earl Shibe Paint Shop in Hammond Indiana to be painted. They advertised on TV regularly, "We will paint any car any color for forty nine dollars and ninety nine cents!" I went there early in the morning and had some of my friends follow me to pick me up. We were going to spend the day having some fun and pick the car up in the afternoon. When I met with the clerk, I picked out the color, baby blue and confirmed the price. He then told me that it would be ready in two hours. That scared me.

I still don't know how they could prep and paint a car in two hours. I told him to please take his time and I would be back to pick it up in the afternoon. The paint job was OK for a three hundred dollar car.

The U.S.A. was in a recession in 1961 and summer jobs were very scarce. I was in college studying business and hoped to find work that was not just labor or farm work. Shortly after arriving home, one of my dad's friends, Ralph Levy who was the regional manager for Fuller Brush Company asked me if I wanted to work as a salesman for the summer. From 1906 until today, Fuller Brushes have been known as the finest quality money can buy. In 1961, Fuller was a household name, known by everyone. Fuller Products were only sold door to door, and many if not most housewives expected to have the Fuller Brush man knock on their doors several times each year. Fuller started out to be a brush company selling brooms, and brushes of all kinds from scrub brushes to tooth brushes.

Over the years Fuller expanded its line to include all types of household cleaning products, inspect repellant, beauty items, car care items and more. Mr. Levy explained to me that Fuller's policy was that their sales force were to be twenty-one years or older and that they were self-employed contractors. Since he had an open territory in the town of Hobart, a blue collar suburb of Gary, he was willing to let me "give it a try" for the summer.

Fuller salesmen carried a "suitcase" that when opened up displayed several dozen products. We knocked on the door and when the lady of the house answered, she was offered a free gift. That was a small lipstick sample, a comb, or a vegetable brush. When they told us which they wanted, we asked if we could come in and open our case to get out the free gift. Most could not resist a free gift. After we opened our case we gave them the gift and told them what our specials were for that day. A large portion of them ordered something and it was off to the next house.

I learned several sales principles that summer. First, persistence pays off. On my first day of training, Mr. Levy parked his car at the end of a street, grabbed the sample case and off we went. There were about ten houses on a block and we had no success in the first block. After knocking on about half of the houses on the second block with no success, Mr. Levy stopped and said, "I'm excited!" I was puzzled and asked why? He said that every house that produced a "no" response moved us one house closer to a yes! A few minutes after that comment we hit pay dirt and secured a nice order. I never forgot that statement.

The second thing I learned was the value of following successful programs. Fuller had a plan and if you worked the plan, success was almost guaranteed. The plan was to start knocking on doors at 9:00 A.M. and keep at it until 5:00 P.M., Monday through Thursday. Friday morning all orders for the week were sent to the warehouse, and Friday afternoon was reserved for delivering the orders for the prior week.

On hot days when success seemed to be non-existent, it was tempting to knock off early and head for the beach, but with a few exceptions I beat the pavement for seven to eight hours a day. If our weekly sales exceeded three hundred dollars we got our products for sixty percent of the selling price. If our weekly order dropped below three hundred dollars we paid seventy-five percent of the selling price, so there was a big incentive to reach the three hundred dollars.

I accomplished the goal almost every week.

My most memorable week was after I had been selling for about six weeks. Mr. Levy was happy with my performance so he sent a trainee to work with me. He was at least ten years older than I, so it was an honor to be selected as a trainer. The first day he worked with me was a Tuesday. About one hour after we started I knocked on a door and the lady said, "I am so glad to see you." She explained that her daughter was getting married in a few weeks and she wanted to order all the products she needed to set up her house. It took over an hour to list all the items she wanted which totaled about three hundred and fifty dollars. By the time we took our noon break we had sales for the morning of over four hundred dollars, more than many salesmen sold in a week.

Every Tuesday all the salesmen that reported to Mr. Levy met for lunch. We took turns reporting our sales for the morning. Needless to say, I enjoyed that lunch very much. My trainee was amazed at how easy this was going to be, and the following week he started his route. As I recall, he lasted about two weeks as he found out that it wasn't as easy as his first day with me. In 1961 the average working man in the U.S.A. made about five thousand dollars a year or one hundred dollars per week. I made far more than that and while I never sold another brush or mop after that summer, sales became my career. Even when I advanced in my career to management, I never forgot the value of making a sale, whether it was selling a product or an idea.

I was grateful to Mr. Levy for taking a chance on me, an eighteen year old farm kid with no sales experience.

In September of 1961 I headed back to Indiana U. It was more of the same as I worked at the girl's dorm and attended classes that were primarily business related. My grades were not what they should have been and I was really not sure what I wanted to do for a career. I decided to take a semester off and put some money in the bank. One of my friends at IU was new to Valpo as his family had recently transferred to Indiana from Pennsylvania. His dad was a production executive at a new steel mill that had just opened on the shore of Lake Michigan, about fifteen miles from Valpo. Almost all of the employees of the new Midwest Steel plant were experienced steelworkers that were laid off from old inefficient plants in Pa., but my friend's dad got me hired as a laborer.

Working in a steel mill was quite an education. I was assigned to the sheet shearing and shipping department. Our plant was a sheet mill which means we produced steel in large rolls of steel that were purchased by the auto industry, appliance industry, and a number of other industries. Some of our customers wanted sheets of steel and others wanted to buy the steel in rolls. Our department was responsible for cutting the rolls into sheets, warehousing the product and loading the trucks and train cars for shipment to the customer.

The warehouse was so big that six or seven train cars could be located inside for loading along with a number of tractor trailers.

One of the first lessons I learned was to not "rock the boat." Most of my co-workers were old enough to be my father and almost all were staunch union supporters. Shortly after I started I was informed by a co-worker that I was working too fast. He advised me to slow down or I would make the rest of the workers look bad. My first month or two, I had two jobs. One was to sweep the warehouse and the other was to paint the equipment. The warehouse had nothing on the floor to sweep, and all of the equipment was new! Basically, I was told to just keep moving.

After I was there a few weeks, I was pushing a broom when I saw a co-worker drive by on a "tractor," a huge forklift capable of lifting over fifty thousand pounds. I recognized him as a guy that started with the company one day after me; a violation of union rules as all job promotions were based on seniority. I told my foreman that I was "older" (union term for more seniority) than the guy on the tractor.

It turned out that the guy driving the forklift was a friend of the foreman. The next day I was driving the tractor and the other guy was pushing a broom. I really liked driving a forklift, but more importantly, it paid more. Laborers were grade two and were paid two dollars and twenty one cents per hour. Each move up the job grade scale was worth ten cents. Tractor drivers were a grade four so I moved up to two dollars and forty one cents. That meant almost one hundred dollars a week in pay.

Working in the steel mill was my first experience at shift work. We operated 24/7 five days a week with three shifts each day. Swing shift meant working 8AM to 4PM one week, 4 PM to midnight the next followed by midnight to 8AM the next. The toughest shift was midnight. You finished your four to twelve shift Friday night at midnight and went back to work Sunday night at midnight. It was very hard to stay awake the first two or three nights. By Friday you were getting acclimated and then it was back to eight to five on Monday.

Working the night shifts meant extra pay, about a five percent premium. At one point I said or did something that ticked off the supervisor who made the schedule. The result was four straight weeks of the midnight shift. That totally ruins your social life. I got home about 9 AM and tried to get some sleep. Doing anything in the evening was not fun as around 11PM it was time to go back to work. The four to twelve shift was even worse. By the time I got off work everyone was home for the night. It was nice to have time off during the day but again, around 3PM it was back to the mill. We had a few guys in our department who preferred to work the midnight shift as there was a lot less supervision and less pressure to get work done. Not me!

Next I learned to be a "hooker." The huge coils of steel, and piles of sheets of steel called lifts, were moved around the warehouse by a gigantic overhead crane. The crane went across the entire warehouse which was about as wide as a football field. It was on large steel wheels like those on a train, and it could roll from one end of the warehouse to the other carrying hundreds of tons of steel. The crane operator was about forty feet off the floor in a cabin attached to the crane.

As a hooker, I worked with the crane man and hooked the coils or lifts to the crane. After the steel was securely hooked to the crane, I signaled for the crane man to raise the load. I then went to the area where the load was to be set down and gave the crane man the signal to lower the load, and unhooked the load. We loaded trucks, trains and constantly moved steel around the warehouse.

One night while I was on the midnight shift, I was working with a crane man named Sal Appa. Sal was a guy with glasses that looked like the bottoms of coke bottles. No one liked to work with Sal as he often missed the mark with the crane and it really caused the hooker to be on his toes. I hooked the crane to a large stack of steel sheets and gave Sal the signal to take it up. He did and simultaneously started moving forward. When the load of steel was about twenty five feet in the air, I heard a scary sound. The sheet lifter started to make a clicking noise that it should only make when I pushed the button to open it. I looked up and saw thousands of pounds of oiled sheets of steel flying through the air like a huge deck of cards being dropped. I turned and ran and heard a horrible loud roar. The load of sheets fell on many stacks of steel and caused a huge mess.

Hundreds of thousands of dollars worth of steel were destroyed. At the side of the mess was a restroom made of cement blocks with no top. Steel came to rest against the open door and it turned out there was a guy in there. It scared him to death. Sal was also very upset as this could have cost both of us our jobs. It was about 3 AM when the supervisors started to arrive to survey the situation. I remember a high level manager ask me if I was sure that no one was under the tangled mess of steel. A head count showed that we were all OK. The immediate assumption was that I had improperly hooked the load. The next day there was a big safety hearing in the executive conference room and both Sal and I were asked to give our side of the story. My description of the clicking noise caused them to investigate the sheet lifter and they found that it had an electrical short causing it to open in the air. Sal and I were vin-

‥ ted but there were some anxious moments. It took several days to clean up the mess. A huge magnet was attached to the crane and the steel was lifted up and loaded into train cars to be recycled.

As I looked back at the situation, if I had not heard the clicking noise and ran, I most likely would have been killed. A modification was done to the sheet lifters that turned the power off before it went into the air.

Once again God was looking after me.

I started in the Steel Mill in January of 1962 and worked as many hours as possible. Of course, any hours over forty were paid at time and a half, or about three dollars and fifty cents per hour. One week when I was on the four to midnight shift, my boss came to me at about 11:30 and asked me to work a "double" as someone due in at midnight called in sick. That meant work a second straight shift and get off work at 8 AM after working sixteen hours, get a few hours of sleep and return at 4 PM. I said yes and the next night at 11:30 he asked me to do it again. The third day it was the same scenario so at the end of the week I had worked forty regular hours and twenty four at time and a half. I was walking dead the third day but the next Friday when I got my pay it was sweet. I got almost two weeks pay in one week.

By that time I had quite a bit of money saved and it was time to get rid of the old baby blue '55 Chevy. Truman Gaines had a beautiful '57 Chevy on his lot. It was a black Bel Air two door with a black and silver interior. It had stick shift and a 283 cubic inch V-8 engine. I bought it and it turned out to be a great car. It was very fast and the only one of its kind in the area. I have had a lot of nice cars in my life but that Chevy was my all time favorite.

In May of 1962, Midwest Steel had a reduction in force and I was among the people who were laid off. In 1962, all young men over the age of eighteen were eligible for the military draft. I was no exception. As long as you were in college full time, you were allowed a deferral until graduation. When I dropped out after my third semester, I moved to the top of the list, and draft day was imminent. I kept in touch with the draft board and informed I would be getting a "Greetings" letter from Uncle Sam within a few months.

I visited the local Army National Guard Armory with several friends and found that there were openings to join the Guard. Everyone who entered the Armed Forces had a six year commitment. If you were drafted you spent two years on active duty followed by two years of active reserves and two years of inactive reserves. National Guard members served six months in the regular Army and then five and a half years in the active reserves. At the time, active reserves meant a meeting every Tuesday and two weeks of training every summer. Eight of us agreed to join the Guard, with one stipulation. We did not want to go to basic training until September which would give us a few months to enjoy some beach time. They agreed and swore us in June with a September date for basic training.

When we joined the United States was not involved in any military conflict. The Vietnam War was in its infancy, but that would change a short time later. By 1964 it was almost impossible to get into a reserve unit as a lot of young men tried to avoid the draft and Vietnam by joining the reserves.

Three of my friends and I decided that it would be fun to live at the beach for the summer. Ed Campbell and Jim Loayza and I found a cottage that was walking distance from the water at Johnson's beach which was a local hangout on Lake Michigan. The beach was frequented by a lot of young people in the area and the bar at Johnson's beach was a lively place. The cottage was owned by an eccentric lady by the name of Lola Lettica. She seemed quite old at the time but I suppose she was in her 60's. She was fond of tee shirts without the benefit of a bra and she had wild hair that looked like it hadn't been brushed or combed for weeks.

The cottage was one large bedroom with four bunk beds and a kitchen/living area all on the top floor. The lower level was unfinished with sand for a floor. She had purchased square cement pavers that she wanted to use to make a floor. The problem was that the cottage was several hundred feet from the closest parking area and it was all up-hill. She told us that if we would carry the pavers up to the cottage she would rent it to us for one hundred dollars per month, half of her regular price. We were all over that and for the first few weeks we lived there we carried pavers up the hill every time we were going to the cottage. We had a lot of fun there that summer.

About the time we moved in, Jim Loayza got very sick and had to move back to his parent's home. They are Christian Scientist so they did not believe in getting medical treatment. Jim was in bed at home all summer. I believe Jim was close to death for a while, but by the time I left for basic training he was getting better. Because of his illness and tremendous weight loss, he could not go to basic training and he got a permanent medical deferment.

Since I was laid off from the Steel Mill, I got a job part time working for Heinold Oil Company at a truck stop in the area. It was open twenty four hours a day and I often worked the night shift. I did not need a lot of income as my share of the rent was twenty five dollars a month and I had no debt. I spent a lot of time on the beach that summer, but by September I was ready to head off to basic training.

CHAPTER 6

Basic Training

My first train ride was my class trip. My second train ride was from Valpo to Fort Jackson. South Carolina. The date was September 9, 1962. To this day I do not understand why the eight guys from Valpo were sent to Ft. Jackson. Everyone I knew from my area was sent to Fort Leonard Wood, Missouri for basic training. One hundred and ninety two members of my basic training company were from Florida, Georgia, Alabama and South Carolina and eight were from Indiana. We arrived in South Carolina in the middle of September, so we avoided the summer heat of the south. It was still very warm during the eight weeks we spent learning to be soldiers.

My first memory of basic was my first breakfast at Fort Jackson. We went to the mess hall and moved our metal trays down the chow line. I saw a pot full of Cream of Wheat and since it was one of my favorites I loaded up. I almost spit out the first bite. It was my first taste of grits. I love grits now, but that was a rude introduction.

Before I left home to go to basic training, I was given advice by several Army veterans. "Never volunteer for anything" and "never make excuses." "Never sit in the front row or in the back row unless you want to be called on." It was all good advice. On our first day of basic training, our sergeant asked for volunteers who wanted to be truck drivers. A bunch of hands went up and a few hours later we saw the "truck drivers" pushing wheelbarrows full of dirt. I now understood why I was told to "never volunteer."

It amazed me that our military has been so successful when I observed some of the decisions that were made. We had a guy in our company that was a professional truck driver in civilian life. He loved driving trucks and made that known to the powers that be. They made him a cook! Several days into basic training about fifteen names were called out during the first role call in the morning. My name was among those called and we were told to report to the orderly room (company office) after breakfast. We were told that we had been selected to be truck drivers (for real) and to load up to go and take a test to get our military drivers license.

On the way, a very nervous guy sitting beside me told me that he had never driven anything. All military vehicles at that time were manual transmission so it was impossible for him to pass the test. He was sent back to the company and most of the rest of us passed with no problem. A truck driver was made a cook and a fellow that had never driven anything was selected to be a truck driver! Amazing.

A few days later I was again told to report to the orderly room. I was informed that I had been selected to be the jeep driver for the Battalion Commander, Lt. Colonel Kennedy. How I was selected from about eight hundred members of the battalion was and is a mystery to me but it really was good duty. On a number of days while my fellow soldiers crawled in the dirt, did P.T. and sat in boring classes I was sitting in my jeep outside Colonel Kennedy's office snoozing.

On one occasion I drove him off base to his home. In general he treated me very well. One day after I had been his driver for several weeks he asked me if I would consider going to Officer's Candidate School. That would have required me to enlist for three years. I politely told him that I was not interested. I suspect my ROTC training was responsible for my good fortune but never found out for sure.

One of the aspects of Basic Training that I enjoyed most was rifle and machine gun training. I fired expert with the M-1 rifle which is the highest possible grade. I enjoyed shooting rocket launchers, the 50 caliber machine gun and throwing hand grenades. By the end of eight weeks with only Army approved food, no candy or soft drinks, no alcohol and a lot of physical training, I suspect I was in the best shape of my life. We were forbidden to walk anywhere out of our barracks. We were required to run everywhere we went. The Army formula to get young men in shape and groomed and organized surely worked.

At the end of basic training we got a few days leave time to go home. They let us grow our hair for a couple of weeks and we were starting to look human again. The morning we were to head home we were marched back to the barber shop for one more head shaving. One thing our Sergeants seemed to enjoy was mail call. We would assemble in formation and they would call out our names. We ran to the front where they were standing to get our mail. Several guys got cookies or other goodies from home. They had to open the boxes in front of everyone and if there was anything to eat in the box, they had to dump it out on the ground.

We had a coke machine at the entrance of our barracks but if anyone was caught getting a coke, they were immediately dispatched to K.P. duty or all night guard duty. They were sadistic people!

When we arrived back at Fort Jackson after our leave, we were ready to head out to Advanced Training. Since my home company was a combat engineer unit, I was sent to Fort Leonard Wood, Missouri for Engineer training. The trip from Jackson to Leonard Wood was my first time in an airplane. It was an old four engine prop plane that was chartered by the Army to move troops around the U.S. It was an ugly pink plane that obviously had seen its better days. The flight attendant (they were called stewardesses) was equally unfortunate looking. After about two hours, we arrived at the Fort Leonard Wood air field. It was a very foggy day and the pilots made two passes at the runway without coming close. They gave up and flew to an airport several hundred miles away and landed without incident. After waiting for some time, we were bused to Leonard Wood.

Fort Leonard Wood is known by its nickname, "Fort Lost in the Woods." It is in the middle of Missouri and also in the middle of nowhere. . Shortly after arriving at Fort L. W., I got a ride home to Valpo and got my '57 Chevy and brought it back to Missouri. We were not allowed to have cars on base, but there was a huge privately owned lot just off base that had hundreds of cars parked for soldiers that were not authorized to have vehicles. The closest city of any size is Columbia, which at that time was the home of The University of Missouri as well as two all girl schools, Stevens College and Christian College.

Advanced training was much less intensive than basic training and weekends were generally free. We were allowed to have weekend leave, but were not supposed to go more than fifty miles from the Fort. Columbia was about fifty miles away so it was a popular getaway spot. I became close friends with another guy in my company by the name of Bob Burriss. Since we had wheels, we left base every Friday night and spent the weekend in Columbia. We came back on Sunday evening. There was a Servicemen's club in Columbia that was a great place to hang out for the weekend. Bob had spent a couple of years at the University of Florida so we were both very comfortable on college campuses.

Near the end of my six month active duty time, I headed home to Valpo for a weekend. It was not a smart thing to do, since we were supposed to stay within fifty miles. I don't know how far it is from Valpo to Leonard Wood, but I would guess it is over five hundred miles. One of my friends from home, Carl Hager went with me for the weekend. On Sunday afternoon we headed back to Missouri. Somewhere in Southern Illinois on the famous Route 66, he asked me if I wanted him to drive. We switched places and continued on our trip.

After an hour or so, I looked up and saw a truck stopped on the road directly in front of us. Carl was apparently having trouble staying awake and did not see it. I screamed for him to stop and he locked up the brakes. We slid into the back of the tractor trailer and stopped with the car about two feet under the truck. When he backed up, we were amazed to see the hood peeled back but no damage to the radiator, headlights or any other part of the car. The truck driver had totally stopped with no lights on and seemed unconcerned that he was stopped on a four lane highway in the dark.

Since we were still well beyond the fifty mile limit and it was about 8 P.M., we tied the hood down and headed toward Missouri without calling the police. Again, God was looking out for us. Oh, by-the-way, that was the end of Carl's driving duty. We made it back to base by midnight but the Chevy would have to wait until I was discharged to get the hood replaced.

Advanced training was much different than basic training. We learned to build bridges, roads and do a variety of construction type jobs. It was said that we went ahead of the infantry to prepare the way. It was an extremely cold winter in Missouri and time spent in the field was not fun. We spent a number of nights in pup tents and on several occasions woke to find snow on the ground. The only heat we had was from drums with wood fires. At the end of the eight weeks of training I was sent to a permanent engineering company to finish my final ten weeks of active duty. That was easy duty and on March 8, 1963, I was on my way home.

CHAPTER 7

Back to Civilian Life

I immediately went back to Midwest Steel and found that I had been called back to work from the layoff. Because I had been in the Military I received my seniority from when I originally started there. One day one of the foremen, a guy named Tom that I liked and respected asked me what I was going to do with my life. He told me that twenty years earlier he had gone to work in the US Steel mill in Pittsburgh and was only going to work there for a short time to save some money to go to college. He said he got married, had children and now was trapped! He told me to get out of the mill and go back to school. I had no intention of staying in the steel mill, but his encouragement to get out was good advice.

I quit the mill and got a part time job working at Roy's Mobilgas. I was living in the attic of my parent's house so my expenses were low. I enrolled at the Gary campus of Indiana University in September of 1963.

In August of 1963 an event that would change my life dramatically (for the better I may add) occurred. It was a Sunday afternoon and I stopped with a friend at the local Dairy Queen on the main street in Valpo. Since I got out of the Army, I had dated a few girls from the area but had not found anyone that I was interested in. While eating my ice cream, I noticed a young lady sitting in a car near mine. Her male companion had gone to get ice cream and I decided to speak to her. I walked over to the car, introduced myself and got her name. It was Diann De Armitt. I had seen her around town a time or two but had never met her. She had just graduated from Valpo High School in May of 1963. I asked her if I could call her, got her phone number and the rest is history! We started dating a few days later.

On one of our first dates I took her to meet my parents. It was a Sunday afternoon and I had just purchased a Colt 32 Automatic pistol. I asked her if she would like to shoot it. She said yes and we went down the hill from our house into the marsh. I found an old metal battery and set it on a stump. I only had eight bullets so I shot four and hit the target three times. I reloaded and gave the pistol to her. She put her four shots in the middle of the battery! I did not know at the time that her dad was an NRA pistol and rifle instructor and that she had been shooting since she was a little girl. From that day until today, I never surprise her!

I loved my job at Roy's Mobilgas. We were a station that never closed. In 1963, there was no self serve gas. Every station had attendants and we cleaned the windshields, checked the oil and put air in tires if asked. In addition to pumping gas, I washed cars, changed tires, did oil changes and other auto service. We were a U-Haul station so renting trailers and trucks was another duty. We also had Avis Rent-a-Cars and three or four tow trucks. Most of the vehicles involved in wrecks in our area were towed to our facility and stored in the lot behind the station. There was never a dull moment and the owner, Joe Kratz was happy to let me work the night shift that allowed me to go to I.U. and study during the day. The station was on US Highway 30, a four lane highway that connected our area with the suburbs of Chicago.

It was interesting work and I met some real characters from midnight to five in the morning. One other benefit that came with that job was meeting and becoming friends with local law enforcement officers. Before the invention of cell phones, the only communication with police was the police radio system. We had police radios in the station so we could know immediately when there was an accident that required a tow truck. We also kept a coffee pot on 24/7.

The Valpo police, the Porter County Sheriff's department, and the State Police all visited Roy's on a regular basis, especially during the nighttime hours. Each officer had his own coffee cup hanging on a hook and there was always a hot pot of coffee at their disposal. While working with Joe, I was introduced to seat belts. Seat Belts were not standard equipment on new vehicles until 1968, so virtually no cars had them. Joe had seen many accidents that resulted in loss of life because occupants had been thrown out so he equipped all of his cars and trucks with seat belts.

One Sunday morning he took me to the "bull pen" where the cars and trucks that were towed in were stored. He showed me a car that he had brought in the night before that was in a head on collision. Both the driver and the passenger in the front seat were killed. Seat belts most likely would have saved one or both lives. I installed seat belts in my Chevy that day.

One of the State Policemen that I liked a lot was Jim Bowe. One night Diann and I decided to park on one of the quiet dark county roads to talk. Soon after we stopped, a state police car pulled up behind us and turned on his flashing light. When he approached my car, I rolled the window down and it was Jim. He said, "Denny, it's you. I saw your dad yesterday. Well, take care." With that, he went back to his patrol car and drove away. He was very embarrassed. That was a funny moment.

Another time Diann and I decided to talk in a quiet place; I drove to a lane on my dad's farm and parked. Actually, it was very close to where my brother Tim now lives. After we were there for a short time, a deputy sheriff who I did not know drove into the field and stopped behind my car with the lights flashing. He came to the car and asked for my license. I asked him why he was bothering me and told him I was on my own property. I told him that if he wanted to go to the farm house and check with my dad he could verify the facts, but suggested he leave us alone. He rather quickly did an about face and took off. I suspect he was hoping to find us in an embarrassing position, but he was disappointed. We actually were talking. That was fun.

In addition to working at Roy's and going to IU, Diann and I were dating on a regular basis. She was enrolled at Valparaiso University and living in a dorm there. Before the end of her first semester she got very sick and had to drop out of school. Rather than return to school the next semester, she decided to get a job at with a local dentist as a dental assistant.

After I finished my six months of active duty my military obligation consisted of a drill every Tuesday evening from 7 P.M. to 10 P.M., and two weeks of duty every summer called "summer camp." Since I had a class at IU on Tuesday evening, I joined a few other guys in my company for Tuesday morning duty. We did maintenance and other odd jobs. After a few months of daytime duty I was called into the office to meet with the Sergeant in charge of our local unit. He told me that the unit was overstaffed and that those of us who were not able to make Tuesday evening drills were being offered the opportunity to go to inactive status. That meant no drills and no summer camp. I tried to hide my excitement and told him that that would be fine. For the next two years I was free. In 1965 I got a surprise.

More on that later.

One day when I was working the day shift at Roy's, Diann borrowed my '57 Chevy for the day. I was working in the shop when I heard my license plate number come across the radio. One of the Valpo police officers called my plate number in to get the name of the owner of the vehicle. I recognized the voice as Johnny Schultz, who was the closest thing in Valpo to Barnie Fife of Andy Griffith fame. He was divorced and single and had a reputation of pulling women over for no reason. It turned out that he did not pull Diann over, but just wanted to find out who she was. The next time he was in the station I had a "discussion" with him and suggested he stick to his job and not worry about who was driving my car.

One of my closest friends at the time was Tom Frailey. He also graduated from high school in 1960 and for the next couple of years had a few jobs but nothing that would qualify as a career. One day we decided to apply for jobs as Indiana State Policemen. The Indiana State Police are one of the elite state police forces in the nation. Most state police are called Highway Patrol and patrol the highways in the state is all they do. The State Police in Indiana are a complete police department with responsibility for all police work, crime solving and prevention etc. We sent in our applications around the beginning of 1964. After a few weeks, we did a written exam. While I was waiting for the next step which was a panel interview, I started a job with Firestone; more on that later. Tom did the interview and then a panel interview. He was hired and retired a few years ago with over thirty years of service as a state policeman.

CHAPTER 8

1964 - A big year!

In February of 1964, Diann and I decided that we wanted to get married. I bought her a ring and it was official. We set our wedding day for August 29 of that year which was a busy day. It was my dad's birthday and my brother Ardie's birthday. In my discussions with Diann's father, he thought it would be a good idea if I got a real job before I married his daughter. At the time I was working for my cousin Jim Heinold, converting old military warehouses into chicken houses.

Early in April, I was between classes at IU in Gary when I took a look at the want ads in the Gary paper. I spotted an ad for a "Retail Sales Manager" at the Firestone store in downtown Gary. At the bottom of the ad it said "Ask for Mr. Wade." A few years earlier when I was working at Heinold and Feller Firestone, there was a guy by the name of Bud Wade that was "on loan" from Firestone. He was sent to help the business get "off the ground." He functioned as the assistant manager and spent several years there before returning to Firestone to manage the Gary store. I called the number and when I told him who I was and that I was interested in the job he had advertised, he told me on the phone "you're hired." I guess his memory of me was a positive one. I went in to the store and met him and filled out an application and he informed me that I would have to go to the Firestone District Office for interviews, but he was sure that I "had the job." He told me that the job paid four hundred dollars per month and that there was opportunity for advancement. I went to the Firestone District office in Chicago and interviewed with several people.

From my time as a Fuller Brush salesman and my time at the Service Station, I knew that I wanted to work in business and that I loved to interact with people. After the interviews in Chicago, I was told to start my new job on Monday, April 13. My first day on the job, I asked Mr. Wade what my hours were. He said that the store was open from 8 AM to 6 P.M. daily, but Monday and Thursday the hours were 8 AM to 9 PM. I again asked what my hours were and he said "I just gave them to you." That works out to about 58 hours a week. I knew immediately that I would have a very difficult time attending school and working this job.

Since I loved the job from day one, I decided that after I finished the semester I would put college on hold. It is still on hold! After a short time with Firestone, I knew that I had looked for a job and found a career. Fortunately, during the time I spent with the company, career advancement was based on performance and not education. Most of my peers, supervisors and the men and women that reported to me had college degrees, but I know of no time when the lack of a degree hindered my advancement.

When Bud told me that I would get four hundred dollars per month, I gave it little thought as that was a decent starting wage in 1964. Somehow I expected one hundred dollars when I got my first weeks paycheck. It was ninety three dollars and sixty cents. I then remembered that there are fifty two weeks in a year and ninety three dollars and sixty cents a week totaled forty eight hundred dollars per year. My hourly rate was one dollar and eighty cents. I got paid for forty hours at regular time and eight hours overtime. There were no wage and hour laws so I probably worked about sixty hours a week on average. I was actually making about one dollar and fifty cents per hour. My primary duty during my time at the Gary Firestone store was retail sales. I learned a lot from Bud who was an excellent store manager. He was very organized and was a skilled salesman, and the Gary store was very profitable under his leadership.

Since I was getting married I decided that I needed a more dependable auto. My '57 Chevy was getting close to one hundred thousand miles and that was a lot for a vehicle in that era. A friend had a "split pea soup green" Chevy with low mileage. By comparison, it was a very unattractive car. As I recall it only had about thirty five thousand miles on the odometer. It had no radio, rubber instead of carpet on the floor, a six cylinder engine and stick shift. I think it was the least expensive car Chevy made in 1960 as it had no options of any kind. It did have a heater. We traded even up! When Diann saw it she was not happy and to this day she reminds me of what a bad trade I made.. I did install a radio. A year later I sold it to Diann's brother and bought a new Pontiac.

ON AUGUST 29, 1964, Diann and I were married at the Emmanuel Lutheran Church in Valpo. Following the wedding we went to Wellman's for the reception which consisted of cake and ice cream. I hid my car at Diann's uncle's house as it was common for young men at that time to do unpleasant things to the bride and groom's auto. It was untouched and we headed for the Holiday Inn in LaFayette for our first night as a married couple, which was about a two hour drive.

We went into the hotel lobby together and the clerk at the front desk asked if we wanted the honeymoon suite. I am not sure how he knew we were "just married" but we said yes. A bottle of Champaign was sent to the room, compliments of the hotel. It was a nice touch.

The next morning we headed south. We had no plans other than to spend a week on our honeymoon. In Kentucky we visited Mammoth Cave. It was an interesting tour of a huge cavern. Diann did not particularly enjoy this adventure, but she was a good sport. The next few days we traveled into Tennessee and spent some time in Chattanooga. We then headed toward Gatlinburg. As we were traveling through the mountains and went through a number of small burgs, we got a bit uncomfortable as we observed the groups of men hanging around the gas stations in each town. We commented that no one back home knew where we were and if we stopped, we might just disappear forever. Just as it was getting dark, we went over a hill and spotted a terrific little resort called Nantahala Village.

It was not uncommon to travel without reservations in those days and when we went in we were able to get a great room. It was a rustic yet high quality place that was the nicest hotel either of us had ever experienced. Remember, I was twenty one and Diann had just turned nineteen. Neither of us had done much traveling other than with our parents so this was a big deal. Many years later when we were living in Florida we went back for our thirty fifth anniversary. Sadly, we found that the original resort had burned but we stayed in the new Nantahala and had a great time. From there we went to Gatlinburg. In 1964 Gatlinburg was a sleepy little town. We stayed there for a couple of days and then headed back to Valpo. We had a great honeymoon, low budget and not exciting by today's standards but perfect at the time.

We returned to Valpo and our new apartment. It was a small one bedroom unit that was attached to a house located about four blocks from the center of downtown. We were the first tenants. Before it was converted to an apartment it was a small machine shop. It had a small bedroom, a small kitchen a bathroom and a nice sized living room. It had wood paneling on the walls and tile floor throughout. It had a small fenced front yard. A garage separated the apartment from the house, which was occupied by Diann's sister MaryAnn and her husband Ken.

Since it was our first home, we had zero furniture. My parents gave us a wedding gift of cash which we spent to buy a sofa, a brown Ethan Allen that cost us three hundred dollars. We purchased a wooden chair and a rocking chair from a local furniture store. Our bed was the bed that Diann had at home and her father gave it to us. It was a frame and mattress with no headboard. I bought an unfinished chest and stained it and that was the extent of our bedroom furniture. Our kitchen had a small table and two chairs that I found second hand. The only item we still possess is the wooden chair. It has been moved about fifteen times and is still in perfect condition.

My favorite part of the new apartment was the garage. When it as built, a pit was installed under the garage that was accessed from the basement of the house. It was great when a vehicle needed an oil change.

Shortly after returning from our honeymoon, I was called into the District Office in Chicago and offered a promotion. In October 1964 I was off to the Michigan City, Indiana store as Office and Credit manager. This turned out to be one of the most difficult assignments of my thirty seven year career. The title of O. & C. manager meant doing everything the manager did not want to do. My primary duties were to handle all of the store reports which were all done manually at that time, and to take care of all items related to credit. At that time, credit cards had not been invented and if you wanted to buy something with extended payments, the decision to extend credit was done by each individual store. In addition to extending credit, my job was to collect weekly and monthly payments from all the customers that bought on credit and repossess any items that were not being paid as agreed. In addition, I did most of the selling. My commute was about the same as the drive to the Gary store, about thirty minutes.

The Michigan City store was an old type store located downtown. The front entrance was a store front with a long narrow showroom. Tires were stored in the basement and there was also storage on the second floor. Tires and batteries were installed in the small service department located on the alley in the rear. Customers would park on the street and come in to buy tires. After the sale was made, they had to go back to their car or truck and drive around the block and enter the service department from the alley. There were two bays and no lifts. The vehicles were lifted by jacks that went under the bumpers. We also had a service truck and a pickup truck to service commercial and dealer accounts.

In addition to tires, the store sold a complete line of appliances, lawn mowers including riders, and bicycles. We sold all kinds of balls, bats, BB guns, rifles and shotguns, golf clubs and equipment. We stocked a complete line of household goods such as pots and pans, toasters, and irons. And Toys! The upstairs was loaded with toys. After Thanksgiving we moved all of the toys downstairs for Christmas sales. In January we moved what was unsold back upstairs.

When I was assigned to Michigan City, the manager was Dean Robison. He usually showed up at about 9 AM, an hour after we opened. The store closed at 5:30 PM and Dean usually left about four to "make deliveries." There was only one other employee who did the service work.

Needless to say this was a lot different than my first assignment in Gary which was a typical six bay auto and service center. I have often said that if I had started in Michigan City I most likely would have quit as it was a miserable situation. A few months after I arrived, Mr. Robison was fired and a new manager assigned. His name was Tom Peacock and he was much different from Robison, but not much better. I later learned that since the M. C. store was such a bad facility, no one with any talent would consider going there as manager.

I became very skilled at repossessing merchandise while there. Seems my predecessor as O. & C. Manager decided that he would get promoted by increasing sales. Both the Store Manager and the O. & C. Manager falsified dozens of credit applications indicating that customers had good credit when they were deadbeats. As a result sales were great as all of the deadbeats in Michigan City headed to Firestone to buy stuff that they had no intention of paying for. Both the manager and assistant manager were promoted to bigger stores in the Chicago area. Shortly after I arrived at the M.C. store, I discovered their scheme. When Mr. Carl Brown, the District Manager found out what they had done they both were fired immediately.

For a number of months thereafter, I spent many hours visiting homes and apartments in the worst part of town and repossessing merchandise. TV sets, stereos, refrigerators, pots and pans, bicycles, stoves, washers, dryers lawn mowers and more. At one point there was more repossessed merchandise in the store than new. I did hire a huge black policeman by the name of Jim Webb to assist me, which made the job a lot easier and safer.

While I was working at the Michigan City store I made my first major purchase. I ordered a 1965 Pontiac Le Mans Hardtop. It had a V8 engine and was blue with a black vinyl top. I thought it was beautiful and the total cost was just under three thousand dollars. That doesn't sound like a lot but when you are making about six thousand dollars per year it was a big deal. When I ordered the new Pontiac, Diann's brother asked me to sell him my 1960 Chevy, but he needed it right away. I sold it to him and for a few weeks while the Pontiac was being produced our family vehicle was a 1937 Buick that I got from a customer of the Gary Firestone store. He needed four shocks and two tires for his truck so I traded him. It was a big tank and not much to look at, but it ran. When the new car arrived, I was a very excited guy.

CHAPTER 9

The Moving Begins!

In June of 1965 I was again called into the district office. I was given an opportunity to move to Chicago to become the assistant manager of the largest store in the district. I was twenty three years old and was excited to get such a responsible position. The store was located at 1550 South Wabash Ave., just a few blocks south of downtown Chicago. The Wabash Ave store was huge. It had three outside salesmen, five service trucks with operators that traveled all over the city installing and repairing truck tires. The service department was a large garage with space to service twelve or more vehicles at one time. It also had a gas island that was very busy.

All told, I believe the store had about twenty employees at the time. When I reviewed the personnel files, I discovered that I was the youngest employee of the store. The manager was a fellow by the name of Dave Walker. It is hard to believe, but I now worked for the third incompetent manager in a row. Dave was a nice man with very limited management skills. How he became manager of the largest store in the District is a mystery.

A few months after I arrived, Dave was history and Wally Nykaza was assigned. Finally, I had a talented and hard working manager to learn from. I learned a lot in my time at Wabash Ave. Our customer base was white collar people from downtown and a lot of low income folks from the south side, one of the worst ghettos in the US.

I met a lot of "characters" during my time there. I also spent some time collecting past due payments on the south side, an area that I would have preferred to avoid. Most of the employees were black and all were much older than me. One of the biggest challenges was my commute. Diann's Mom was dying from cancer at the time. When I got moved to Wabash I decided that I would not move Diann to Illinois while her mom was alive, so I commuted by train. I walked from our apartment to the Pennsylvania train station and boarded the train at 6:00 AM. The ride to downtown Chicago was about ninety minutes. When I got off the train, I took the bus to the store and usually arrived shortly before 8:00 AM. At the end of the day I reversed my trip and arrived home about 7:30 PM. On Saturday the store closed at noon. I then took the South Shore RR, an electric train and arrived in Chesterton Indiana about 2:00 PM, where Diann picked me up.

Martha De Armitt passed away in September of 1965. Shortly after she died, we packed our belongings which were few, and moved to Park Forest, Illinois our first move. For the balance of the time I worked at Wabash Ave., I took the train from Park Forest to the store which was a short forty five minute commute.

As mentioned earlier, I was enjoying the inactive reserve status from the military. For about two years I did not hear anything from Uncle Sam. In September of 1965 I received a letter from the Department of Defense. It stated that I had two choices. Find a reserve unit to serve in or be called up to active duty. Neither choice was very appealing but the first one was the better of the two. I contacted my local unit only to find that they had no openings and a waiting list for men who wanted to join. Vietnam was now in full force and joining a Guard unit meant only six months of active duty and most likely no time in the war zone.

I finally found a Transportation company in East Chicago, Indiana that had an open slot. Since I was qualified to drive vehicles up to five tons, they were willing to accept me. For the balance of my six year obligation which was about three years, I attended meetings one weekend a month and two weeks every summer. I received an honorable discharge in July of 1968.

In January of 1966 I once again was called into the District office. I was informed that there was a new store opening soon in the suburb of Hillside, Illinois. It was a twelve bay store in a shopping center and it was to be a seven day a week store. I was asked to go there as the assistant manager and since the manager of the new store was in charge of another store, my job was to set the store up, hire the employees and when it was ready to open, Mike Walker would arrive as manager. Mike was a friend that worked at the Gary store when I was hired. He trained me as Office & Credit manager and we got along great.

I accepted the position and started working at Hillside in February of 1966. It was a great learning experience and in April of 1966 the new store opened. It was a success from day one, and Mike was an excellent manager. My commute to Hillside was by car and the downside was that Diann was without a vehicle and had to take the bus to her job as a dental assistant.

CHAPTER 10

My first Management Assignment

In May of 1966 I once again was called into the District Office. During the prior year I completed my store manager training program which allowed me to work for a week in Mishawaka, Indiana and a few days in a store in Wisconsin. I was now being offered the "opportunity" of managing the Gary, Indiana store where I began my career just over two years earlier. This would require us to move back to Indiana after about a year living in Illinois.

The good news was that I would get a company pickup to commute and I was able to commute from Illinois for a few months. I was to be on salary for the first time, a massive six hundred and fifty dollars per month plus bonus. I was twenty three years old and to be assigned a store manager position at that young age was very unusual. The Chicago District was comprised of about thirty stores and I was the youngest manager in the district.

There was some bad news. Bud Wade was promoted to a new store two years earlier and he was replaced by a guy by the name of Don White. Don was part of an experiment by Firestone Management that hired college grads and put them into an "accelerated" program. Normally, it took about two to three years for a person to go through the process of becoming a store manager. It took me twenty six months. The college training program allowed a person to become a manager in six months from date of hire.

The program was a complete failure and I am not aware of one person who was in that program that was successful. Don took the Gary store from Bud Wade and in about two years turned it into a complete mess. His last year in Gary resulted in a loss of over thirty seven thousand dollars, a huge amount in 1965. That made Gary the third largest loser in the entire USA! In addition, the facility was allowed to deteriorate and was in very bad condition. Of the five lifts in the store, three were out of commission.

I was excited to be given such a great opportunity and worked long hours cleaning and organizing the store. Guys that were good employees under Bud had gone downhill and were problems that had to be addressed. One technician, Sammy Beck was very skilled but had gotten into some very bad habits. He was habitually late for work, came to work hung over, and missed a lot of days. He was a very funny guy. One day when he arrived for work he was battered and bruised I asked him what happened? He said, "I was broadcasting when I should have been tuning in".

His downfall was on a day he arrived late for work. When I told him that it had to stop he told me that the store could not be profitable without him. That was the wrong thing to say to me. The next time he was late he was terminated. During my first year in Gary, I had to replace almost every employee.

While I began my career with Firestone without any long term goals, managing a store was a job that I loved. The Gary store was a challenge in many ways. In addition to the normal retail tire and service business, we provided truck tire service both at the store and on the road. We had three service trucks that were equipped with air compressors and could repair or replace tires anywhere. We also had one large truck that could handle the very large tires on earth movers and the huge trucks that moved products at the steel mill. Some were over seven feet tall and weighed over thousand pounds. During that era, many tires were sold by service stations and we also sold tires to them.

For the first year or so I took care of all the sales of truck and dealer sales in addition to the retail sales. I opened the store at 8 AM every morning, worked late many days. We closed at 6 PM every day except Monday and Thursday when we were open until 9 PM, and I closed the store almost every day. I probably averaged about seventy five hours a week at the store. As time went on I hired and trained some very capable employees and was able to scale my hours back. I also changed the hours so we closed every day at 7 PM which was a better fit for both our customers and our employees.

When Harvey Firestone opened the first Firestone Store in 1928, his concept was for stores that sold not only tires and car service, but complete home and lawn and garden products, a one stop shop. The Gary store sold TV's, radios, lawn mowers and lawn supplies, refrigerators, freezers, bicycles, wagons and many other small home and garden items. This created several problems. One, I had almost zero interest in these products. I loved cars and almost anything related to cars but selling and delivering a freezer just did not excite me. I felt that the time it took to assemble a lawn mower was counterproductive.

A bigger problem however was the fact that the Gary store was downtown and within a few blocks of some of the nastiest ghettos in the entire country. Many of the folks that bought these big ticket items like TV's and refrigerators sometimes "forgot" to make their payments. That meant sending someone to collect payments and if that could not happen we had to repossess the items. Bud Wade taught me that when you went into the ghetto to collect or repossess, act like you owned the block and never to appear to be afraid. Sounds good, but not so easy to do.

The worst problem with the home products was that some of the young men in the area preferred to do their shopping between 1 AM and 4AM. Since we were not open at that time, they usually just knocked out one of the big windows in the front and helped themselves to as many TV sets they could load up in three or four minutes. During the first year I managed the store I got fifty after hour's phone calls from the police informing me that the alarm was going off. I got up, dressed and headed for the store while the police waited for me. When I got to the store I turned off the alarm and called the company that boarded up windows. I was on a first name basis with several of the local cops as well as the boarding guys. By the time the boarding was finished, it was usually about 5 AM so I stayed at the store.

The most interesting experience was one early morning when I got the dreaded call that the store alarm was sounding. I arrived at the store to find two policemen waiting for me. We went inside and I took inventory of what was stolen, a total of about ten TV sets. The policemen then asked me to come to their patrol car and showed me a TV in the back seat. They said the burglars apparently dropped it outside by the alley. They told me that they were having some kind of benefit for the police dept. and would it be OK if they used the TV for a prize. They said my insurance would take care of it.

I told them that it would not be OK and to return it to the store. They were not happy, and I guess I took a bit of risk by calling them on it. The next day at about 9:00 AM, I got a call from a nice old lady that lived in the apartment building just across the alley from the store. The alarm had awakened her and she watched as the bad guys quickly hauled the merchandise from the store. She also observed the cops carry a TV out and put into the back seat of the patrol car. I asked her to call the police station and ask for the officer in charge of the shift and tell him the story. She did and shortly after two very sheepish cops came in and apologized for their actions.

I often wondered how that situation would have turned out if she had not made that call.

IN ADDITION TO BECOMING a store manager in 1966, two other big events happened. About the time I was assigned to the Gary store, Diann found out that she was pregnant and that the baby would be arriving in early 1967. We also decided that it was time to buy a home. We decided to return to Valpo to house hunt and found a nice three bedroom house that was about a thirty minute commute to the store. It was on a quiet street and had a big yard. The asking price was nineteen thousand and nine hundred dollars. We made an offer of seventeen thousand and five hundred dollars and it was accepted. The down payment was two thousand dollars leaving us a loan balance of fifteen thousand five hundred dollars. With taxes and insurance included, the monthly payment was one hundred twenty eight dollars and thirty five cents. That sounds very small today but with my new salary being six hundred fifty dollars a month; there was not a lot of money left over at the end of the month. We were excited to be homeowners and the prospect of being parents also was an exciting time. We had enough furniture to get by. We added a washer and dryer and a riding lawn mower, all purchased from Firestone at store cost.

1967 WAS AN EXCITING YEAR with several big events taking place. The first was a massive snow storm. When I left for work on a Thursday morning, January 19, it was snowing heavily. The store was jammed with customers all morning, all wanting to purchase snow tires. Late in the morning, I made a trip to the Gary Post Tribune newspaper to drop off a newspaper ad and found the going very slow, even with a truck with large snow tires and a bed full of weight. By about 2 PM, we could no longer get cars in and out of the store as the snow had accumulated to about eighteen inches. The street in front of the store was packed and the cars were going nowhere fast. I sent my employees home, but four of us did not get out in time and were stuck at the store. We went to the grocery store down the block and bought some food, but the pickings were slim. Microwaves had not been invented and we had no way to heat food. Since we had pulled the trucks into the bays, the other three guys slept on the seats of the trucks. I slept on the customer lounge chairs. Before going to sleep, I watched the ten o'clock news from Chicago and the weather man assured us that the snow would stop during the night and the plows would be working all night so the morning commute would be slow but otherwise OK.

When we awoke on Friday morning, the snow was thirty eight inches deep. The only vehicles that were moving were snowmobiles, and they were doing emergency duty for people with medical issues. There was no way to plow snow as there was no where to put it. We were really in a state of emergency. I was able to contact a customer who had a front end loader and he arrived on Sunday to clean our parking lot. The streets were cleaned by loading the snow into dump trucks and dumping it in Lake Michigan. The trucks worked twenty four hours a day Friday, Saturday and Sunday and well into the next week. By Sunday night I was able to slowly make my way home to Valpo. The same conditions existed there. Diann's dad walked to our house which was about two miles from his home and she walked back with him. She was in her last month of pregnancy so getting into town was important. It took about a week for things to return to normal and then another large storm hit. It was not nearly as big as the prior storm, but just caused more inconvenience.

The second big (huge) event of 1967 occurred about two weeks later on February 12. Stephanie Lynn came into the world. Needless to say, our lives changed dramatically. She was a happy healthy baby and we enjoyed being parents. I was not in the delivery room when she was born (not allowed in 1967). Diann was a great mother and did one hundred percent of the diaper duty. I changed a few wet ones, but when the diaper had foreign matter in it I passed. On one occasion when Di went shopping I was watching Steph when she put a load in her pants. I debated whether to wait for Di but decided that might not go over too well. I took her to the back yard, removed the diaper and washed her bottom with a garden hose. That did not go over too well when the mom found out what I did. At least it was summer time.

Sometime after her birth, we decided that it was important that we get back to church. Since we married two plus years earlier, our church attendance was spotty at best. After her birth we started attending church on a regular basis. In the spring time both Diann and I accepted Jesus Christ as our Lord and Savior. That was a big change for us as we joined the Apostolic Christian Church and were baptized on July 9 along with my cousin Glen Pfeiffer. As I mentioned in Chapter 1, the A.C. church as we called it was very conservative.

For the next twenty years we would struggle with many of the practices of the church. It is full of wonderful people, kind and generous and they were very faithful to the church. Unfortunately, many were very religious but didn't seem to have a relationship with Jesus. They often were motivated by fear rather than love for the Lord. I am thankful for the foundation I received in that church and am also thankful that I was able to move to another church where I was motivated by what would please the Lord rather than fear.

Diann got herself pregnant again in 1968. David Allen was born early in the morning on May 29, 1969. Diann had some complications with the delivery and was taken to intensive care to get her blood pressure regulated. About 6:30 in the morning, I was told that all is well and she was moved to a regular hospital room. I then made what seemed to be a good decision at the time, but looking back it was somewhat questionable. I dropped Stephanie off at my parent's house and headed for Indianapolis 500 race with three of my cousins. We had great front row seats on the start/finish line and we smoked cigars as we witnessed Mario Andretti win his first and only 500.

While Mario and I are not great friends, I have spent quite a bit of time with him in recent years and it was neat to tell him that I saw his victory at Indy. I have been reminded a time or two of my somewhat dumb decision, but Diann was a great sport and never punished me for it.

A short time after David was born, Di was pregnant again. This time it did not work out well. After about four months of the pregnancy her doctor told her that something was not right. He was unable to detect a heartbeat and feared the baby was not alive. That did turn out to be the case and the next few months were very difficult for her; more on that later.

As a store manager, a number of opportunities opened up to us. One was the opportunity to participate in sales contests. In 1968 the company announced a seven day contest trip to Acapulco, Mexico. With a lot of hard work from my team, we managed to win the trip. At the time there were about one thousand Firestone stores in the USA and seventy five of us won the trip. There were a lot of district managers, and home office people on the trip as well. It was Diann's first plane ride and I still remember her fingernails digging into my wrists as we took off. We flew to Dallas and the next day three chartered jets full of Firestone employees and spouses headed for Mexico.

It was a fun filled week with great food and sightseeing. There was only one problem. August in Acapulco must be the hottest and most humid place on the planet. The hotel had to put large blocks of ice in the pool to keep it cool enough to use. The air conditioning in our room was barely adequate, but to a twenty six year old farm kid and his twenty four year old wife it was unbelievable. Shortly after we got home we were in another trip contest. We won that one also and went to the Bahamas in the spring of 1969. Diann was very pregnant with David on that trip, but since it was in March it was a great time to enjoy the warmth of the sun.

The sales and profits at the Gary store continued to grow each year. After I had been there about three years I got a phone call from the District Manager, Mr. Carl Brown. He told me that a college junior from Purdue had been hired for the summer intern program. He said that the store would only be charged for half of his salary so I was getting a full time employee for about three months at half price. He then said, "Oh, by the way, the student is your younger brother." Ardie worked with me for the summer and as I recall we had a good time.

Needless to say, he chose a different career path than tires but the summer of selling tires and service in Gary was good experience. By year four we were one of the top five stores in profit in the Chicago District. I loved the job of store manager and really had no big desire to advance beyond that position.

Sometime early in my fourth year in Gary, Diann got a call from Mr. Brown. He invited us to join him and his wife for dinner the following Saturday night. He was a great District manager and I admired and respected him. We drove to Chicago that Saturday and went with Carl and Ruth to the Acacia Country Club for dinner. That was a venue that we were not familiar with. We had a very nice dinner and after dinner Carl told Diann that with every good TV show you have some commercials and this was no different. He told her that I had a lot of potential for advancement with Firestone and that I could be promoted to his staff in the near future. He also told me that to be promoted I needed to find and prepare someone as my replacement as store manager.

I found out later that he had heard that I was considering leaving the company to go into business with Lynn Feller in a new location in Crown Point, Indiana. Lynn had taken me to lunch one day and proposed that as a possibility but I had no real interest. Carl did a good selling job that night. A few months later he was promoted to the corporate headquarters in Akron, Ohio and a young guy by the name of Jack Gallagher replaced him.

I must have done an OK job because shortly after he came to Chicago, Mr. Gallagher called me into the District office and offered me a promotion. It was May of 1970 and the Chicago District had grown to over thirty company stores and a number of additional stores were planned. As a result, the two Store Supervisors were challenged to keep an eye on all of them and the decision was made to add a third supervisor and that was me. After a meeting with Mr. Gallagher, I flew to Akron to meet with the top management of Firestone. After two days of interviews with a lot of Firestone executives, called going "through the chairs," I was approved as a Store Supervisor.

CHAPTER 11

Store Supervisor

The new assignment meant a number of changes. First, we had to move to a Chicago suburb as my new office would be on the south side of the city. My stores were primarily in the city with a few in the suburbs. We were able to sell our house in Valpo rather quickly and moved to a small three bedroom ranch in the town of Woodridge Ill, a western suburb.

As I mentioned earlier, Diann was pregnant with our third child and about the time we were preparing to move we were informed by her doctor that there was a problem. No heart beat was detectible. She was about five months into the pregnancy and the baby was apparently not alive. There was nothing that could be done, but wait for her body to reject the dead baby. Needless to say, the next few months were very, very hard for us.

We moved to a new state, I had a new job that was very demanding, and Diann was at home with two small children and no support system. The new doctor in Illinois said that we should not travel far from a hospital as she could go into labor at any time. When she was full term, it was obvious that the baby was not alive and in fact her physical appearance did not show any signs of a pregnancy. The doctors determined that it was time to remove what was left of the baby. She went into the hospital and was given a large amount of a drug that would cause her to abort. It did not work, so they surgically removed it. That night I got a call from her doctor asking me to come to the hospital immediately. She had gone into a coma from the drugs and they were very concerned. The doctor later confided in me that he was concerned that she might not make it through the night.

Thankfully she suffered no physical problems from the ordeal. The bad news is that she did struggle for some time with depression that we believe was directly related to the pregnancy and loss of the child. She found a great Christian psychiatrist that helped her through the ordeal. We were thankful that we had two healthy children and her doctor who was a Catholic advised her that she should avoid future pregnancies.

My new job was much different from my job as store manager. For the first time I would be managing "from a distance." As a store manager, I could give my employees goals and assignments and follow up on an hourly or at least on a daily basis. My first day on the new job I reviewed the personnel files of my twelve store managers. I was twenty eight years old and I discovered that all of my managers were older than I was. I was concerned that some of them might resent me because of that, but that never became a problem. My group of stores was not performing well and I spent long hours six days a week hiring, training and working with my employees. I loved the challenge and I enjoyed the sounds and excitement of the city.

I often reflected on the fact that just a few years earlier I was a farm kid and was so thankful for the opportunity Firestone and this great country gave me. During the two years I was on this assignment my stores went from a dismal position to the number one profit group in the entire USA. There were about seventy five groups in the country at the time so that was a major accomplishment. As is always the case, my managers and their employees were responsible. I just tried to put the right people in place and got out of their way.

We also won our next contest trip during that time, a trip to Jamaica. We left Chicago in January when the temperature was twenty below zero. We flew to Jamaica and arrived in seventy five degree weather. We stayed at the Playboy club in Ocho, Rios and it rained almost every day we were there. It was warm; the trip was free so no one complained. One of my memories is playing volleyball in the pool in the rain. On our last day we were told to put our suitcases out in the hall by 4 AM so they could be taken by truck to the airport. Unfortunately, I packed the shoes Diann was planning to wear home. She went to breakfast, rode the bus to the airport, walked across the tarmac to the plane and flew to Miami barefoot. After we cleared customs in Florida we were able to open our suitcase and find her shoes. She was not happy!

CHAPTER 12

Corporate Headquarters

After twenty four months as supervisor of the stores in Chicago I got a call to come to Akron Headquarters to interview for a new assignment. The job was titled Western Division Retail Sales Manager. The country was divided into five sales divisions and the Western Division started in Chicago and included Districts in St. Louis, Milwaukee, Minneapolis, Fargo, Kansas City, Denver, Omaha, and Oklahoma City. Each of these cities had a District Manager and two or more Store Supervisors, the position I previously held in Chicago. The Division Retail Sales Manager was usually a somewhat temporary position that was a steppingstone to the position of District Manager.

I was offered the job and accepted it with June of 1972 the start date for the assignment. We put our house in the Chicago suburbs up for sale and it sold quickly, in less than a week as I recall. We moved to Wadsworth Ohio, a close suburb of Akron and bought a four bedroom split level house. It was much bigger than our prior two houses. It was a nice home but not very attractive. We knew that it was likely that we would be moving again within a year or two.

This job was my most difficult from a family standpoint. Again, Diann was moved to a new city and since my closest District office was Chicago, I traveled three or four nights a week almost every week. On several occasions I left town on Sunday night and returned Friday. Saturday was an office day so I had Saturday afternoon and Sunday to prepare for the next trip. My job was to work directly with store supervisors who were struggling and especially to spend time with them in their losing stores. I enjoyed the challenge of this assignment, but because of the constant travel, I looked forward to the day I could get my own District. I did have lots of fun getting familiar with the cities in the Midwest. The St. Louis district was one of our worst so I spent a lot of time there.

One Monday morning I was walking through the Akron Canton Airport when I spotted my boyhood idol, Stan Musial sitting on a stool at a counter having a cup of coffee. Turns out he had been in Akron to play Firestone Country Club over the weekend and was on his way home to St. Louis. I approached him and asked him if he had ever played any baseball. He smiled and said that he played a little bit. He was very friendly and gracious and we had a ten minute conversation. So many famous people are arrogant and unapproachable and I was so happy to find him the opposite. Stanley Frank Musial, "Stan the Man", a great baseball player, but an even greater man passed away in January of 2013 at the age of 92.

During our short stay in the Akron area we attended the Apostolic Christian Church in Akron. While it was the same denomination as the Church's we attended in Indiana and Illinois, it was much more conservative and legalistic.

While living in Wadsworth I purchased a real cool car. I ordered a new 1973 Pontiac Grand Prix, black inside and out. It was a great looking car, a two door hardtop with a big V8 engine and my first vehicle with air conditioning.

CHAPTER 13

Moving On

On a Monday morning in early 1973 I had boarded a plane for St. Louis when the flight attendant (we called them stewardesses in the old days) looked at my ticket and told me to go back off the plane and call my office. There were no security lines, no metal detectors, and no seat assignments. You often boarded the plane and gave your ticket to the stewardess. I went to a pay phone, called my boss and he told me to come to the office.

The airline got my bag off the plane (imagine trying to get that done today) and I drove to the office in Akron. I was sent to meet with the V.P. of sales who told me that there was a District open in Hartford, Ct. and he asked if I was interested. I said I was and went back to the airport to fly to New York to meet with a Mr. Jack Benner who would be my new boss. He was the Eastern Region Manager, responsible for the dealers and stores in the Northeast USA. After an interview with him and a quick lunch, I flew home.

When I walked into the house later that afternoon, Diann was a bit surprised as she assumed I was in St. Louis. I informed her that we were moving again, this time to New England. I was assigned to the Hartford District where I was responsible for about forty stores throughout the New England states. The Hartford District was next to the worst in the USA in profitability.

Overnight travel was a lot less, but I worked long hours to improve the performance of the district. We bought our first new home, a four bedroom colonial on an acre of land in the historic village of Somers

Ct. We loved living in Connecticut, and formed some great friendships. Wayne "Kup" and Marcia Kupferschmid and their family became dear friends. We spent a lot of time with them during our year in Connecticut and Diann and Marcia are as close as sisters. Kup and I have had many wonderful times on golf courses all over the country.

There is a large apostolic church in Rockville, Connecticut and we attended there while we lived in CT. It was the most conservative church we had attended and I guess they did not know what to do with us so they pretty much left us alone. We did make a lot of great friends there

CHAPTER 14

Headed South

Unfortunately, the 1970's in corporate America were lean years and Firestone like many other companies did a lot of consolidation to reduce costs. Exactly twelve months after taking over the Hartford District, I got called to Akron headquarters. The Hartford District was being closed and merged with the Boston District and I was sent to Atlanta to take over another struggling district which encompassed most of the state of Georgia, as well as parts of Alabama and South Carolina; another move, another house to sell, and tears, as we said goodbye to our new good friends. We bought another new house, a beautiful two story brick home. We again became very fond of our new home and fell in love with the "south."

Living in the South was a new and wonderful adventure. I loved the weather with no snow to shovel and our location in Duluth (pronounced doo-luth) was a thirty minute drive to Atlanta where my office was located. It was also near lakes and mountains, a truly beautiful area. We learned about boiled peanuts, eating field corn rather than sweet corn and collards. We also quickly learned that it was preferable to be from Indiana rather than Connecticut, and that the south was going to rise again. In 1975 there was no love for the folks in the northeast. Indiana seemed to be OK. We also learned that the Civil War that we briefly studied in school was a very important topic in the South. We learned that the official name for the war in the south was and still is "the war of northern aggression."

For the most part, locals were friendly but at arm's length. It is understandable I guess since thousands of people from all over the country were settling in Atlanta in that era and in many cases the local people felt they were being invaded. I learned the difference between a Yankee and a Damn Yankee. A Yankee came south to visit and a Damn Yankee came south and stayed.

One particularly fond memory was the time I went to Walhalla, South Carolina to visit with Bum Long and Newt Collins. They owned a long time Firestone Dealership in a small town just outside Clemson, SC. They were real down to earth mountain men, very rough around the edges, but kind and warm. My first visit as the "new" district manager was shortly after I was assigned. Jack Brown was my assistant and together we called on them. Jack told me to plan to spend the night. After a visit to their dealership, we headed to their rustic cabin on a nearby lake for dinner. Ol' Bill, an elderly black gentleman came to the cabin and cooked us dinner, filet mignon, baked potatoes and all the trimmings. Jack and I spent the night and the next morning was a great surprise. The cabin was on a fifteen acre lot which was all planted with azaleas of every shape, size and color. Growing azaleas was Bum's hobby as well as a nice source of income. Acres of azaleas, in full bloom, were one of the most beautiful sights I have ever seen. Before we left the next day, Bum invited me to come back on a weekend with my family and bring a trailer to get "some azaleas." A few weeks later I rented the biggest U-Haul trailer I could find and headed up to visit "Bum and them" as everyone in the office referred to them.

When we arrived at the dealership, Bum took a look at the trailer and asked how I was going to haul anything in that little trailer? When we got to the cabin, we found two of his workers had dug about forty azaleas, some as tall as six feet. I was thinking one gallon pots and he was thinking ten year old azaleas that were like trees. We loaded them on the trailer and got them all home with no problem. Again, Bill came to the cabin and cooked us a wonderful steak dinner and told us food for breakfast was in the refrigerator. It was typical of southern hospitality, something that the rest of the country could learn from. As a young guy from a distant land, I had several similar experiences while in Georgia.

While we loved living in Atlanta, my job as Atlanta District Manager was not so good. My office was in a large complex with a number of offices and a large regional warehouse. The Southern Division Office was in the same building and my boss, Carl Hart was just down the hall. He was a very sadistic and mean person, and some of the things he did to the men who reported to him were very demeaning.

I spent most of my time out of the office visiting my stores and dealers, but often had to interact with him. After I was on the assignment for about eleven months, he was demoted and moved to Tampa as District Manager and the Southern Region was closed.

He eventually was fired; something that rarely happened to someone who had achieved the level of management he had reached. Obviously, during a thirty seven year career I had some difficult days and some difficult weeks and months, but my year in Atlanta was my only difficult year. Since I was able to complete thirty seven years with the company and only one was very difficult, I was truly blessed.

The Southern dialect was something we found interesting and sometimes frustrating. One day Stephanie came home from school very frustrated. I believe she was in the second grade and her teacher told her to close the winder. She did not know what a winder was (a window) and as a result her teacher got upset with her.

David was a five year old and he made great friends with a neighbor, Marshall Dericott. He was a police officer, he had a motorcycle and Dave loved to spend time with him.

During our year in Atlanta, we were blessed with a lot of visitors. Folks from both the Midwest and from the Northeast often stopped on their way to Florida. We often just changed the sheets on the guest room bed in time for the next visitors. During our time there my parents stopped and spent some time with us. During that visit we learned that my dad was not feeling well and at that time the doctors did not know what his problem was. He was only about fifty five years old and we hoped that it was nothing serious, but it was the beginning of his battle with cancer of the pancreas.

CHAPTER 15

A Sad Day

Sadly, twelve months after arriving in Atlanta, I got a call to fly to Akron. It was not good news. I met with Larry Lombardo and Tom Mertz. They were the Vice-President and Executive Vice President of Sales for the entire company. They told me that the company was reducing from about eighty Districts nationwide to forty. I was told that the Atlanta district was being closed and consolidating with Charlotte. Al Hall was the Charlotte District Manager and he would be in charge of the new district. Needless to say, I was not happy.

I told them that they were making two mistakes. One, the new consolidated District should be in Atlanta and two; I should be the District Manager, not Al Hall. I was being asked to move back to Akron headquarters to take a new assignment until another district became available. Not only would I have to move again, our house in Hartford was still not sold. Moving to Akron and buying a new house would mean I would be the proud possessor of three houses. Today when a company like Firestone asks someone to move they purchase the employee's house. Back in the olden days, they had a convoluted plan. They paid the principal, maintenance and taxes on the old house and gave the employee a loan for the down payment of the new house. That plan was for six months after which you were on your own.

The company actually purchased my house in Connecticut as part of the deal which moved me to Akron. Soon after, the company announced the plan that I believe is still in place today where the company buys the house to take the burden off the employee. Looking back on the situation, we moved from Chicago to Akron to Hartford to Atlanta to Akron in a period of thirty months! We bought and sold a house each time. That was very, very tough on the family. I loved my work and was amazed that an Indiana farm kid with no college degree could climb that high that fast. I felt that my work ethic and dedication to the assignment would allow me to continue to grow with the company so I did not even consider leaving the company.

Once again, Di went willingly to Akron but she did shed some tears along the way as we really loved living in Georgia.

Moving to Akron meant I would again be on the road a lot covering the eastern third of the U.S. We spent the next seven years living in Northeast Ohio. David and Stephanie spent most of their school years there and we developed some great friendships. The Ritzmans, Spanglers, and the Grafs were great families and we spent a lot of time with them. Our next door neighbors, Tom and Doris Grammas were also great friends.

It was during our time in Ohio that my dad became very sick. During the time we lived in Georgia, my parents came to visit and it was the first time I was aware that Dad was not feeling well. After we moved to Ohio, he was diagnosed with cancer of the pancreas which is probably the worst possible type of cancer. His treatment was surgery to lessen the pain and suffering, but there was not much else that could be done. He did make a trip to the Mayo Clinic in Minnesota to see if there was anything they could do. I flew to Minnesota and drove Mom and Dad home after that visit. He did have some good days and actually did some farm work the year before he passed away.

During the last few months of his illness we made many trips to Valpo to see him. Diann stayed with him and mom when it was obvious that he would not live much longer. During his last week, he called Stephanie and David into his room and told them that he wanted to see them in heaven.

He passed away at home on May 25, 1976. I have several memories of his funeral. First was the number of people who visited the funeral home. As I recall, visitation was from 2-5 PM and from 6-9 PM. There was a line out the door of the funeral home all afternoon and we had a short break to eat. The evening visitation was similar - a line all night going well past 9 PM. I had a number of people tell me that Dad was one of their best friends. He lived in the LaCrosse, Kouts, and Valpo area from the time he was a youngster until his death. He touched a lot of lives during those years and was loved by everyone that knew him.

The line of cars that went from the church to the cemetery was the longest I have ever seen.

Shortly after moving to Ohio, I took up the game of golf. One day when my boss, Jack Benner and I were talking, he encouraged me to get into golf. He said the culture at Firestone included golf and eventually I would have the opportunity to use golf to entertain customers. So I got on the waiting list at the Firestone Country Club, one of the finest and most famous golf facilities in the country. It was located in South Akron, about ten miles from our house and three miles from my office.

In a few months I was notified that I was a member. Firestone Country Club is a golf club with no tennis or pool. It had a wonderful restaurant and two world class golf courses. It was only open to Firestone employees and retirees, and the best part was the cost. No initiation fee and a monthly charge of twenty eight dollars. There was a limit of six hundred members and everyone was treated equally, whether an hourly tire builder or a vice-president, the rules were the same. The head pro was Bobby Nichols, a tremendous golfer who won a number of times on the professional tour and won a major tournament, the PGA.

Diann and I both decided that if we were going to play the game we would take lessons. I inquired about lessons and was given an appointment with Paul Lazzaro, the assistant pro. Diann on the other hand was given lessons by Bobby Nichols, who apparently preferred to teach women, particularly good looking women. David and Stephanie were introduced to golf at FCC, playing in the junior golf program each week. While neither of them was particularly interested in golf at the time, today they both enjoy the game.

A few years later, we got sad news as Firestone Tire and Rubber Company sold the Country Club; more on that later. During two recent trips to play at Firestone, I had the opportunity to see Paul and catch up.

While living in NE Ohio, we learned the winters were long and since we enjoyed being outdoors our family learned to ski. We took lessons at a small bump of a hill called Brandywine for six successive Sunday nights. We took a number of ski trips to Michigan, Colorado, and New York during our time there.

We also took two memorable trips while living in Akron. The first was a ten day trip to the Western USA. We bought a new 1978 Oldsmobile Station Wagon and made a big circle going through the badlands of the Dakotas, visiting Mount Rushmore, my sister Laurie in Denver, Diann's Sister Maryann in Oklahoma and her brother Paul in Illinois. We stopped at many sites such as Dodge City, Kansas and had a tiring, but great trip.

Our other family trip was also memorable. Along with my cousin Keith Heinold and his wife Suzie and their two children Mike and Mindy, we rented a motor home and the eight of us headed from Akron to New England. I could write a book about this trip. I learned why you often see motor homes parked at motels! They can get very confining after a few days. Add to that the fact that our rental had a lot of miles on it and was not in great shape. The holding tank leaked which spread our waste across the highways and byways. It was 1976, the bi-centennial and traffic in New England was fierce. Driving a car in Boston is an adventure - driving a thirty foot motor home was a riot. We camped on Cape Cod, walked the Freedom trail and overall had a great time.

The kids got along fine, but that was our first and last motor home adventure. Mike and David had a memorable time on Cape Cod when they stumbled on a nude beach. They quickly returned to where the rest of the family was to get Keith and me to take us to "the show." Needless to say, most of the folks who were on the beach with no clothes would have looked a whole lot better if they had some clothes on.

About six months after we moved from Atlanta to Akron, I got the call to move again. For the first time in my career I got a promotion and did not have to move. I was assigned as the Cleveland District Manager, with my office across the street from the Cleveland Airport. It was about a 45 minute drive from our home in Wadsworth, but the fact that I could commute and we did not have to move again was a huge plus. The Cleveland District was the consolidation of the Cleveland and Akron Districts. It covered the northern half of Ohio and included Cleveland, Akron, Toledo and Youngstown. Not a very exciting area, and all four of those cities were in economic distress.

I was now responsible for about fifty stores and a number of large independent dealers. Since Firestone Corporate headquarters was in Akron, my district was in the spotlight at all times.

During the time I was assigned to the Cleveland District, the famous Firestone "500" radial tire recall occurred. To this day no tire company has ever had a recall so large. It began in October of 1978 and when it ended several years later over seven million tires had been recalled.

It was the beginning of the end of The Firestone Tire and Rubber Company.

Harvey Firestone founded the company in 1900 and for seventy plus years it was one of the most successful and respected companies in the U.S.A. The massive recall was so costly in dollars and reputation that it became necessary to sell the assets a few years later; more on that in a later chapter. The recall was big news, and was a lead story in every night on the local news. With only three or four TV stations, everyone knew about the recall. One day I got a call from a local news reporter who told me he was coming to my office to interview me about the pending recall. I quickly left for the day as I had no desire to be interviewed.

For the first time in my fourteen years with the company I did not tell people who my employer was unless I had to. I believe to this day that Firestone was unfairly forced to recall the "500" by the US government. While there were problems with the quality of the "500", millions of perfectly good tires were recalled and destroyed. I spent four years on the Cleveland District assignment and during that time the district went from the bottom of the list to a profitable and good performing unit.

WHILE WE WERE LIVING in Wadsworth I purchased my first sports car. When I was about thirteen or fourteen years old, my neighbor Ernie Miller had an MG TD that he bought when he was discharged from the Army. I thought it was a very cool car and I always had a goal of buying one someday. I located a 1953 MG TD in Oneonta, New York, and I rented a trailer and Di and I drove there to take a look at it. Even though it was in dismal shape, partially disassembled and had not run for years, I bought it for twenty eight hundred dollars and hauled it to Ohio.

After about two years as Cleveland DM, I was enjoying my job and things were looking good for the future. Diann and I decided to look for some property in the country where we could build a new home. While our last three houses were new, all were spec houses that were under construction when we bought them. The last two were on small lots with close neighbors. We decided that we would like some land and found a beautiful five acre lot that was about twenty minutes closer to my office. We bought the land for twenty five thousand dollars and contracted with Art Graf, a man we attended church with to build us a home. We put our house in Wadsworth on the market and began the process of building. We were very fortunate to sell our house shortly after we began the new house. We found a rental nearby that was barely adequate and we lived there for about three months while the new house was being finished. The rental was built by a local builder by the name of Musch, pronounced "mush," and naturally we named it the mush house. Art turned out to be a great builder and we loved our new house near Medina. We paid Art one hundred and twenty two thousand dollars for the house and when we finished with landscaping, driveway etc. we had one hundred and fifty thousand dollars invested.

My friend from Illinois, Dana Tauffer who was a landscape architect came for a visit and while he was there he did a complete landscape design for the property. Diann and the kids helped me with the project of landscaping. After the lawn was seeded, we spent a lot of hours picking up rocks and tossing them into a ravine beside the yard. One day while we were picking rocks, David managed to throw a rock in my direction. It hit me in the back of the head and I went down like a "rock". An accident I am sure!

While we were living there, I tackled the job of restoring my 1953 MG TD. I removed everything from the frame and rebuilt it from the ground up. I had the engine built by a professional in Cleveland and the body work was done by a local body shop. With a little help from friends, I put it all back together. I finished the job on a Friday and on the following Monday Di and I loaded up our gear and headed to New Hampshire for the annual MG "Gathering of the Faithful." This is an annual event that attracts over one hundred MG's built before 1955.

In retrospect, I was somewhat crazy to head out on a thousand mile trip in a twenty five year old sports car that had just been restored. The good news is that the only mechanical problem we had was that the starter failed. It really did not pose a problem as I was able to park on hills and start it by rolling and popping the clutch. On a couple of occasions I had to use the auxiliary crank. Our neighbors and friends Mitch and Bobbie Mitchell had an identical car and we made the trip together. The weeklong trip included an overnight stop at the Kup's in Connecticut.

That was the first of a number of long trips in the MG, something that we enjoyed very much. The MG is still in my garage and though we don't take a lot of long trips, we still enjoy the wind in our hair. (What I have left.)

Stephanie had a great experience while living in Ohio. She had several babysitting jobs while in Wadsworth, but moving to the house in the country left her with no customers. I was aware that Tom De Leone, the all pro center for the Cleveland Browns lived about a mile away on the same road. I read in the newspaper that his wife had recently given birth to their first child, a little girl. I encouraged Stephanie to write her a letter and tell her that she was certified and experienced as a babysitter. She did not get a reply, but several months later our phone rang and it was Mindy De Leone calling. She asked Steph if she was interested in a job as a mother's helper. Of course she said yes and she watched the baby a number of times while Mindy did housework and yard work. Eventually they left her at home with the baby while they went out.

Steph and David spent a lot of time with the De Leones and other members of the Browns, and she became a huge Browns fan, and continues to support them. It has meant a lifetime of pain as the Browns have been one of the worst teams in the NFL.

While living in Ohio, Dave found his love for sports, and specifically for basketball. He played on his first organized team, practiced constantly and even shoveled the snow off the driveway so he could practice.

CHAPTER 16

Eastern Region Manager

Not long after we moved to our new home, I got a call to once again visit the corporate office of the VP of Sales. There I met a man by the name of Bob Heinlein. It was re-organization time again and Bob had just been brought into Akron to become the new Vice President of Retail Operations, in charge of all of the company owned stores in the U.S.A. He had formerly been in charge of the West Coast Division. He told me that the country would be divided into two regions and he offered me the job of East Coast Region Manager. It meant that I would be in charge of about ten Zones covering all the territory east of the Mississippi river.

The best news was that I would not have to move as the new retail store group would be headquartered in Cleveland. That was obviously good news - a promotion without a relocation. I thoroughly enjoyed working for Bob. While earlier in his career he had the reputation of being very hard and demanding, he obviously had transformed during his career. He was fifty seven years old when I met him and the two years I reported to him were most educational and enjoyable. He was very professional and a smart retailer.

During that time Firestone went through a major transition. From 1900 when Harvey Firestone founded the company until 1980, Firestone was led by a C.E.O. who was part of the family. Every top executive for eighty years grew up in the organization. The Firestone "500" recall that I mentioned earlier changed that. The company was in such bad shape financially that the board of directors went outside the company to hire a C.E.O. In 1979 they chose John Nevin, who had been a V.P. at Ford Motor Company and then the C.E.O. at Zenith.

While I obviously have no proof, I think the Board of Directors hired him to get the company in shape to sell. What I do know for sure is that big changes came to the company. During the two years that I was Eastern Region Manager, we went through a transition from traditional tire stores to stores that were clearly more focused on auto service and customer satisfaction. We also began a remodeling of all stores, a process that took a number of years. I traveled continually leaving home most weeks on Tuesday morning and returning on Friday afternoon.

In July of 1982, Mr. Heinlein called me into his office for my annual review. I had been on the assignment for about two years and the performance of my Zones had continually improved during that time. He gave me an overall excellent rating and told me that he planned to retire in a year or two and that I was his choice to replace him as Vice President of Retail Operations. That obviously was good news. Little did I know what was to come.

CHAPTER 17

Back to Connecticut

Two months later I was again called into Mr. Heinlein's office. He told me that as of that day I was no longer Eastern Region Manager. Of course I was shocked because of what had transpired two months earlier. He could not give me a good reason and said that the decision had been made. I knew that the decision had come down from above him and he was just the messenger. He told me that I would be moving to Cincinnati to become the Zone manager there. He assured me that I would not suffer any pay cut but would have to move. I told him that I would think about it, but that I was not pleased and would consider taking severance pay.

It was the first and only time in my career that I was demoted and no one would tell me why. I was told only that Paul Dolan, my counterpart in charge of the Western USA was being demoted also, and that there would be two new people replacing us. It would be many years later that I would find out the real story and why it happened; more on that later.

A few days later I told Mr. Heinlein that I would not go to Cincinnati, but would consider going back to Hartford Connecticut as Zone manager of the New England states. The Zone Manager who was there was my friend Orland Wolford. He was a Midwest boy who I had assigned to New England and he was eager to get back to Ohio so the switch was made. Unfortunately, to rub salt into the wound, real estate values had plummeted in Ohio and we lost a lot of money on our home. The net result was that we moved into a much smaller home in

Connecticut, one that needed a lot of work. It did have an in ground pool that we enjoyed greatly every summer. We did make a large profit on the Somers home four years later.

Stephanie was a sophomore in High School when we moved and I do not think she ever got acclimated to Somers High School. David on the other hand was in the seventh grade and he only had one question when we said we were moving. Did they play basketball in Connecticut? When I said yes he had no problem making the move.

While I was very disappointed by what had happened, after a few days I made the conscious decision to make the very best of the situation. I guess I was determined to show company management that they had made a big mistake. The Hartford Zone included all of New York, New England and Northern New Jersey, about one hundred stores. I worked hard and the performance of the Hartford Zone was very good. All things happen for a reason and lots of great things happened as a result of the move back to New England.

One of the benefits of moving to Hartford was the opportunity to live near our best friends, the Kupferschmids, Kup and Marcia. We spent a lot of time with them. We again attended the Apostolic Christian Church in Rockville Ct., and had a number of close friends there. Rich and LaNae, Aberle and Doug and Carol Moser became close friends as well.

SHORTLY AFTER MOVING to Connecticut we purchased a Red 1960 MGA car to go along with our MG TD. It was Diann's car and she enjoyed driving it during nice days. It was bright red with wire wheels, a sharp little car. Diann was working at Swiss Laundry at this time and this car was her "purchase."

Unfortunately the MGA met an untimely death. One day she was on her way to pick up David at Somers high school when going over a speed bump caused the batteries to short out and start a fire behind the seat. By the time the fire department arrived, the entire car was on fire. Fortunately the insurance company paid us the full amount we had paid for the car.

DURING THE TIME I WAS in Hartford I won a sales trip which was a four days at the 1984 Olympics, sponsored by Sports Illustrated. Diann and I stayed on a cruise ship in L.A. and watched a number of great events. One memory is that we were in the fourth row watching boxing and Diann spent most of the time we were there working on her knitting as she did not want to watch the sweat and blood. We got to sit next to Doug Collins at an Olympic basketball game. Doug was an outstanding NBA player who a couple of years later became the coach of the Chicago Bulls. In addition, we saw water polo, swimming and diving. Overall it was a terrific trip.

When we returned home a memorable event happened at our home. After a weekend pool party, the water in our swimming pool was about eight inches low. Before I went to work I put the garden hose into the pool and turned on the water. I calculated that it would take about three hours for it to fill. I should note that we had a well and I was concerned about its health. At 10 A.M. I called Dave and asked him what he was doing. He said that he was watching the Olympics. I told him to get up and go turn off the water. He was down in the family room so the trip to the faucet was only about thirty feet away. He said OK and I again said, "Go do it right now."

Diann returned home from work later that afternoon and when she went to the back yard she found the hose in the pool and the water flowing over the top and down the hill. She called Dave and he turned white! He got a bucket and tried to bail out the excess water. Needless to say, I was not happy when I came home from work that day.

The years we were in Ct. were Dave's middle school and high school years and several interesting events took place. Another vivid memory was when he was about fourteen years old. He asked if he could spend the night with a friend. Since that was a somewhat common occurrence we said OK. Sometime after midnight the phone rang. It was the Enfield Police Department. Enfield is a community about ten miles from our home. The police wanted to know if we had a son who was a runaway.

Seems that all three boys told their parents that they were spending the night at one of the other boy's home and they went to the mall. When the mall closed they headed for a park and that is where the police found them. I headed to Enfield and picked him up. On the trip home I did not speak to him, choosing to wait until the next morning to discuss the consequences. He told me later that he had a hard time sleeping that night contemplating what the punishment would be.

I don't remember the exact nature of the punishment, but suffice it to say he did not pull that stunt again.

During the time I spent as Zone Manager in Hartford we won several other sales contests and Hartford was consistently one of the top performing Zones in the country. Thirty years later that is still the case. I would like to think it is because of the foundation I built and the people I hired. One of the men I hired was a young college grad by the name of Dan Artzeroniun. He recently retired from the position of

New England District Manager. That district leads the country in sales and profits consistently.

Another interesting trip developed while we were living in Hartford. Holiday Inn announced a deal that turned out to be a great one for someone like me who traveled overnight a lot. Anyone who stayed seventy five nights in Holiday Inns during a one year period could receive seven nights free in any Holiday Inn in the world, including air fare to get to the hotel. Since I was spending two to three nights a week out of town, I took the challenge. It was close, but by the end of December, 1984 I accomplished the goal. Since the same credit was given if you stayed one night or several, I frequently moved from one hotel to another close by. I spent a lot of time in the metro New York area and in some cases I got three stays in one week by moving each night. Holiday Inn obviously did not make the rules as tough as they should have and the program ended after one year.

Diann and I discussed where to go for our free week. I suggested Japan since the air fare and hotel there would be a huge price if we went the normal way, paying for the trip. Di had always wanted to go to England and so it was to England we went. It was our first trip to Europe since up to that time all of our travel out of the U.S.A. was to Mexico, Canada or the Caribbean. We flew to London and had a great week touring the city and some of the nearby cities. After our week was up, we took the train overnight to Edinburgh, Scotland and spent a few days there. On the train to Scotland we met a lady from Washington D.C. by the name of Valerie Bucher who was on vacation with her daughter. While in Scotland we bumped into her two times and when we boarded the train back to London we again were on the same train. What a coincidence.

It was while we were living in Connecticut that we had several major changes in our lives. After Stephanie completed her junior year in High School she told Di and me that she did not want to go back to high school. The thought of my daughter being a high school dropout flashed across my mind. Actually, she had approached her principal and Baypath College and had arranged to start college one year early. She had earned extra credits during her three years of high school and only lacked Senior English for graduation. We told her that she could go to Baypath provided she lives at home which she agreed to do.

During the fall of her second year at Baypath she attended a dance that included the cadets from the Coast Guard Academy. It was there that she met a young cadet by the name of Jon Beyer that was in his last year at the academy and they had a few dates before she brought him to our house for Thanksgiving dinner. After he left Diann told me, "you have just met your future son in law." While he seemed like a nice young man I was not so happy to hear that, as she was just eighteen years old and in her second year of college.

Diann was right as early the next year he asked me if he could marry Steph. They could not get married until he graduated from the academy in May as any cadet that got married while in school was immediately expelled. So, my daughter who turned 19 in February was going to get married in May and move somewhere in the world with her new Coast Guard Ensign husband. Three months to plan a wedding was not much time. Steph continued to attend Baypath and Diann worked full time, but they put together the wedding in that short time.

Our first thought was to have the wedding at our church, but we were advised that the Rockville A.C. church did not permit weddings unless the couple was members of the church. We then inquired about having the wedding in the Family Life Center which was another building behind the Church. That too was denied.

Sometime during the prior year, Kup, Rich, Doug and I began meeting every Tuesday morning for a bible study and Diann had started meeting with some of her friends for a bible study. As I look back at the situation we both were reading and studying the bible for the first time in our life. God was working in our life and we were not happy with our church.

When we were told we could not have our daughter's wedding there we considered worshiping somewhere else. The pastor at Somers Baptist Church agreed to allow us to hold the wedding there and we left the Apostolic Church and began worshiping there.

Jon and Stephanie had a beautiful wedding in May and the reception was held at our home. It was a lovely day and the yard was in full bloom. The caterer set up his "kitchen" in our garage and a trio played music by the pool. It was a perfect day. I will say that I underestimated the work necessary to have an event of that magnitude at our home.

Jon completed his academy career graduating number one in his class. Cadets got to choose their first assignment based on class rank. Jon got to choose first and he chose to go to Hawaii and serve on a boat that was based in Honolulu. That meant that a few days after their wedding Jon and Steph headed west. Needless to say, that was not easy, especially for the mother. In September 1985 we had an eighteen year old daughter in her second year of college and nine months later she was married and living in Hawaii.

In early 1986, my Supervisor at the time, Keith Weir came to spend a few days with me. One morning we had a long breakfast during which he gave me some interesting information. As Region Director in charge of the Northeast U.S.A. he was charged with identifying the person most qualified to replace him if he were to move to another job. He gave my name to Larry Lombardo, who was his boss and the Vice President of sales. Mr. Lombardo told him to choose someone else because I was not eligible. I really respected Keith as he told me that I might want to look for a job at some other company as based on Mr. Lombardo's comment I would likely have to spend the rest of my career at that level.

Mr. Lombardo was the same person who told Mr. Heinlein to demote me a couple of years earlier. Keith told me that he would hate to lose me if I were to leave, but that I was too young to be locked into my position when he felt I could and should have more responsibility.

An interesting thing happened later in 1985. Keith called me and said "sometimes you bite the bear and sometimes the bear bites you." He told me that his counterpart in the Southwest Region in Dallas was going to resign. That man was Larry Jordan and he was leaving Firestone to accept a management position with another company. Keith told me that I was going to get a call from Larry Lombardo offering me the job replacing Jordan. I reminded Keith that a few months earlier he had told me that I was "stuck" at my level and that Larry Lombardo was the guy who told him that. He laughed and said that apparently they had done a nationwide search and my name came up as the person most capable which was Keith's evaluation earlier.

Sure enough, a day or two later I got a call from Mr. Lombardo asking me to come to Akron. When I inquired as to why I was coming to Akron, he said it was to discuss an opportunity. I asked what the opportunity was and he said he would rather discuss it in person. I told him that I did not want to waste the companies' money and his time and that I would like to know what it was about. He finally told me what I already knew - that the Southwest Region was available. I told him that I was not interested and that I was happy in Hartford. To say the least he was surprised and he then told me that this might be my last opportunity to "move up." That did not go down so well and my response was that if Firestone did not want my services I was sure there were other companies out there that would. Silence on the other end of the phone!

This was the first time in my twenty plus years that I turned down a promotion. A move to Dallas would have meant moving David in the middle of his high school time and that did not make sense to me. In retrospect I am certain that a part of me wanted to take the job, but I guess I wanted to make a statement - that I was not just going to dance to their tune.

In September of 1996 I again got a call from Keith. This time he asked me to grab the next available plane to Philadelphia where he lived and to plan to spend the night. I did so and that night he took me to dinner and told me that he was going to resign the next week. He said that he was sure that I again would get the phone call asking me to come to Akron to discuss the job. The next day we went to Hershey, Pennsylvania and spent the day talking and looking at the hundreds of autos at the annual Hershey show, the largest antique auto show in the world.

I flew home with a dilemma on my hands. We had lived in Connecticut for four years and enjoyed our home and friends. David was just starting his junior year in High School, and was a standout player on the Somers High School Basketball team. If in fact I was offered the job of Regional Manager and did not accept it, my advancement would likely not be considered again. As Keith predicted, Larry Lombardo called me a few days later and again asked me to fly to Akron to meet with him. I did so and he offered me the job. I explained my family situation to him and asked for a few days to discuss the situation with Diann. He agreed. Again, Di said she was willing to go wherever I needed to go. David was another story. In addition to being very involved in Basketball, he had a girlfriend by the name of Emily. He was sure that they would be married some day and was not at all interested in moving to Pennsylvania.

He reminded me that when we moved to Connecticut I told him that he would be able to graduate from High School there. In a recent phone conversation with Keith Weir, he reminded me that David said he would "stay in Connecticut and live in a cardboard box if necessary, but was not going to move!" I then negotiated a deal with Mr. Lombardo. I would take the job if I could stay in Connecticut for David's junior year and then move to Philadelphia. He agreed to cover my living expenses in Pennsylvania for that period of time. He told me the salary that the job would pay and I declined the offer. He then was able to figure a way to increase it to a number that I was satisfied with.

My prior moves with Firestone were all done with career advancement my top priority. This move was the first in my career that was done after much prayer by both Diann and me. I was comfortable with my situation in Connecticut and would have been happy to stay there. It was also during my time in Connecticut that I received several contacts from headhunters who had interesting offers from other companies in the automotive industry.

CHAPTER 18

Northeast Region Director (aka Zone Manager and Zone VP)

After a lot of discussion and a lot of prayer, I decided to accept the offer and on October 1, 1986 I started the new assignment, Northeast Region Director. The title had previously been Northeast Region Vice President and during my twelve years on the assignment the job title changed several more times. The Northeast Region included all Firestone Stores from Northeast Ohio, Cleveland/Akron to the east and from Canada to North Carolina on the South. When I took the assignment the Region included two hundred sixty five company owned Firestone stores. The fact that the job was in Pennsylvania and the residence was six hours away in Connecticut made for a tough seven months.

Most weeks I left the house early Monday morning and returned on Friday evening, attending David's basketball games meant a lot of extra driving. I missed some of his mid-week games, but did manage to get back to Connecticut for most of his Friday games. Somers High School had a very good team that year and they reached the state finals for class S schools. Unfortunately, they lost that game but it was an exciting season.

Time went fast and in the spring of 1987 we began construction on our new home in Pennsylvania. It was a four bedroom colonial on a two and a half acre wooded lot. Included was a two car detached garage for my 2 antique M.G. cars. Our goal was to convince Dave to move with us to Philly and to finish his high school career there. Needless to say, that did not happen. He spent the summer after his junior year living with our great friends, Kup and Marcia. Since they did not live within the Somers school district, he had to move into Somers to enroll for his senior year. We arranged for him to live with neighbors who had a son in his class and who were also on the basketball team. It was a very hard time, especially for Diann. Within a very short time her Daughter moved to Hawaii and David was six hours away and still in high school.

Again, we made a lot of trips to Connecticut to watch the Somers basketball team and we were in the audience when he scored his one thousandth point. He was voted the Most Valuable player in the conference and first team all state, both great accomplishments. As soon as he completed his senior year he moved to Pennsylvania to spend the summer.

Just two weeks after his graduation we got very bad news from Connecticut. John Gibbs, the boy who David lived with his senior year was killed in an auto crash. Another friend and classmate who was driving was ultimately sentenced to prison for vehicular homicide and driving drunk. Two families devastated because of alcohol. Very sad.

Shortly after we got settled in Pennsylvania we began the process of looking for a church home. After visiting several churches we settled in at Windsor Baptist Church. It was an old church, established in the 1800's and we were warmly welcomed. I joined the choir and after a short time there began teaching an adult Sunday school class. About a year after we got there I was asked to join a quartet that needed a baritone. We sang at church functions and occasionally at other churches. Windsor had an active pre-school and not long after we settled in, Diann became a teacher. She continued to teach there for the next ten years and loved it. She has some great stories as three year old kids tell it like it is. During our time at Windsor we made some great friends. One of my great memories at Windsor involved our pastor emeritus Dean Hegerty. Dean had been the senior pastor at Windsor for years and when we arrived there he was about seventy five years old and pastor of seniors.

One Sunday when our Senior Pastor was on out of town I finished teaching my Sunday School class and was about to go into worship service when Dean stopped me in the hall. "I need you to open the service, read the scripture and pray." Since the music had started, I had zero time to prepare. I told him it would have been nice to have some time to prepare and he said "brother, you always need to be ready to preach, pray or pass away." Obviously I headed for the pulpit. I have repeated that quote many times in the twenty five or so years since that day.

During our time at Windsor, we had an opportunity of a lifetime. The Billy Graham Crusade was scheduled to come to Philadelphia for a weeklong crusade. It took place at Veterans Stadium where the Eagles played football. Many months before the event, Diann and I and a number of other members of Windsor Baptist gathered with a bunch of folks from other area churches for our training. We spent a number of evenings with the advance team from the Graham organization preparing for the event. We learned that we would be on the field when Mr. Graham gave the "invitation" and we would be the people who would spend time with the folks that were making decisions for Christ.

We went to the stadium four nights that week and had some great experiences. I also sang in the choir, which was made up of hundreds of people from churches all over the Philadelphia area. That was an awesome experience. The crusade was very successful with hundreds of folks committing their lives to Jesus. Each person was referred to a local church and we had two new families attend and join Windsor Baptist as a result.

David spent the summer working for the Firestone regional warehouse located near our home. Again, we tried to convince him to attend college in Pennsylvania, but he returned to Ct. to attend Western Connecticut State University where he played on the basketball team. Four years later he graduated with a degree in finance.

Early in 1987, we flew to the Big Island of Hawaii for a company trip. Jon and Stephanie were able to fly from their home in Honolulu to join us for a few days. After the company trip was complete, we flew to Maui and met Rich and La Nae Aberle and Kup and Marcia for a few more days. It was a great trip.

Not long after we moved to Pennsylvania we were notified that we were going to be grandparents. Just a year after Stephanie and Jon were married, she gave birth on June 13, 1987 to Caleb, our first Grandchild. Diann flew to Hawaii for the birth and stayed for a few weeks to help Steph. David and I flew to Hawaii shortly after he was born to meet him. Not long after he was born, Stephanie and Jon visited a church near their home.

What happened soon after surely qualifies as a miracle. Stephanie was alone with Caleb one night and she called us. She was very anxious and asked us to pray for her. We were in bed and quickly got up to pray that someone would come to comfort her. We knew no one in Hawaii so prayer was our only means of support. Sometime early the next morning she called us to tell us what could only have been arranged by God. A man and a woman from the church they had visited were out making calls on people who had visited their church. They had not had much success and decided to make one last call before heading home. That last call was on Stephanie.

They invited her to attend their church again and before they left her they prayed with her to accept Jesus Christ as her Savior. She called us again with the good news. God indeed does provide our needs.

During my thirty seven years with Firestone and Bridgestone, I spent a lot of time on airplanes and in hotel rooms. Travel can be fun and interesting and it can also be tiring and monotonous. In addition to my business travel, Diann and I had the pleasure of going on a number of trips, compliments of the company. During my first twenty years or so, the trips were a result of sales contests that I had won. When I got promoted to Region Manager, I attended all of the sales contest trips as a host. The trips that I won prior to my move to Philadelphia were Acapulco, Mexico, several to the Bahamas, Jamaica, Hawaii, the Olympics and several cruises.

During our twelve years in Pennsylvania, we had many great trips including Hong Kong, London, Hawaii, Charleston, The Monterey Peninsula, Phoenix, New Orleans and several more cruises. Since these trips were usually one hundred or more couples, we met Firestone people from all over the USA, and a number of times traveled with people we had met before. Great memories.

Several other trips stand out as special. In February of 1988 we flew to Cancun Mexico for a vacation with our friends, Kup and Marcia, Bob and Barb Ritzman and Rich and La Nae Aberle. We had a great time in the sun with the highlight being the bus trip from Cancun to Chichen-Itza Una Maravilla. It is the Mayan village that has been abandoned. There is a pyramid like structure that the four guys and Diann climbed to the top. What Di did not think about was the trip down. The stairs were very steep and the steps were only a few inches deep and about a foot high. Since she is afraid of heights, making the climb was not a good decision!

I thought I might have to hire a helicopter to rescue her but while at the top we discovered that some thoughtful soul put a chain on the back side. Rich and I "walked" her down backwards. I understand that the Mexican government has now closed this venue to the public. It was really a dangerous place and a fall would probably have meant death!

Bob flew his plane to Mexico so the guys got to go for a sightseeing flight. Dinner one night at a restaurant called Bogart's was a wonderful experience. I believe it is one of my top ten dinners of all time.

As I mentioned in a previous chapter, the 1970's and 1980's were difficult times for Firestone. The "500" tire recall cost the company millions of dollars and was responsible for a much reduced market share. The factories continued to pour out tires that were not being sold. Many dealers that had been exclusive Firestone dealers had taken on other brands so they could offer the consumer something other than Firestone. The company was in bad financial shape in 1979 when John Nevin became the new CEO. While I believe Nevin had the sale of Firestone in his plans all along, the deal was actually announced March 17 of 1988.

I recall going into the office early that morning and checking the teletype machine for messages. (This was before the internet kids) The headline that day was that Bridgestone had agreed to acquire Firestone Stock for sixty dollars per share. As I recall, the stock was selling for around thirty dollars so stockholders were thrilled. I did own some stock and did make some money as a result. The Japanese are very concerned with appearance and they announced the transaction as a merger. In reality it was a takeover with Firestone ceasing to exist as a company. In the beginning it was called Bridgestone/Firestone in all documents and transactions. Twenty five years later it is Bridgestone USA. I believe that Bridgestone paid too much for Firestone. The company was in bad shape with outdated factories and stores that were worn.

In the end, however the move to take over Firestone while costly and difficult put Bridgestone in the position that they are in today. When they bought Firestone they were a small company with almost no presence in the West. By purchasing Firestone they now had factories on every continent and by 2010 Bridgestone had surpassed Goodyear and Michelin to become the largest rubber company in the world.

The merger did cost a lot of Firestone employees their jobs, especially in the production area. I was part of what was termed "Senior Management." That included the top one hundred Firestone executives in the world. Within about six months over half of that group either retired or were asked to leave. The press release said that they "left to pursue other opportunities." I was fortunate to be in the retail division of the company.

Bridgestone expertise was manufacturing and they soon transformed the Firestone factories to the Japanese style. They had almost no experience in retailing so those of us that managed the Firestone Stores were not in any danger of losing our jobs. In fact, several years after the buyout several of us went to Japan to advise them in the area of tire and service retailing. Mr. Ono, Bridgestone CEO stated that while "Bridgestone did not originally want the retail stores, they came with the deal, and now we know that the stores were the crown jewel of the acquisition."

I had twenty four years with Firestone when the buyout happened and I continued with Bridgestone for thirteen more years. While it took a while to understand the Japanese culture, I found the experience to be great. At Firestone it was sometimes stated that long term planning was deciding where to go for lunch. At Bridgestone we had a one year and a five year plan. I am told that the top corporate people have a fifty year plan! It was a sad ending to a great company, but something that had to happen.

Golf had become my number one hobby after "getting hooked" while in Akron. When in Connecticut I joined a private country club and enjoyed playing there. Once I moved to Pennsylvania, I found the area to be full of great golf. After becoming friends with a gentleman by the name of Bud Hughes, I found out that he was a member of Whitford Country Club, one of the best clubs in the area west of Philadelphia where we lived. He and another member recommended me as a member and we joined a year after we moved in. It was a great golf course and we met a number of people there who became friends.

In July of 1988 we flew to Scotland to meet our friends, Ron and Sandy Hanson for a week of Golf and sightseeing. While Ron and I played a number of the great golf courses including The Old Course, Muirfield, Turnberry and Royal Troon, Sandy and Diann toured castles and gardens.

The gals did find out that sexism was alive and well in Scotland when they were asked to leave the Royal Troon golf club parking lot. They were waiting in their car for Ron and me and a little man came out and told them to park across the street and wait for us. Women were not allowed on the property! I think Diann's favorite thing was the sheep that were on the road in the rural areas. Driving on the wrong side of the road with a right hand drive car with stick shift was fun too. We had no room reservations. We stayed in a number of Bed and Breakfasts including one that was a dairy farm. While we had a couple of rainy days, overall the weather was very good.

Rhine River in Germany

IN SEPTEMBER OF 1990 we flew to Germany for a twelve day trip. Since Diann's mother was born there and my ancestors were from there also it was a special trip to learn a little about our past. We flew to Hamburg and rented a car before heading to Einbech to visit Diann's relatives. Her mom's cousin and his family welcomed us with open arms.

Diann took German in school and that was very helpful. While visiting her relatives we took a day trip to East Germany.

The wall had come down shortly before our trip so the trip to the east was the first for her family as well. We went to a concentration camp where the V-1 rocket was built and saw the ovens where the Jews were killed. It was a very somber time. The most amazing thing was the lack of visitors to the site. We learned that the German people were in denial. One lady we talked to told us that it was a lie and that it had never happened. After three days with her family we moved on. We drove all over the country and enjoyed visiting castles and a number of other sites. One day we went into France and toured Alcese Lorrain where my Grandfather Bucher was from. We did not find France welcoming and we were glad to get back to Germany.

We then headed south to spend a couple of days in Switzerland. My mother's grandfather Heiniger came from a small village so we headed there. It was a beautiful little village with cows grazing in nearby fields. The cowbells rang constantly as they moved - a delightful sound. We stopped at the only inn in town and asked if they had a room. We were told no until Diann explained that my ancestors came from there. We then got a room - we were the only guests.

The next day we tried to find someone who we could communicate with. No success. Diann's limited German did not translate in Switzerland. I went to the post office to try to find someone who could speak English. No luck. I did find a number of Heinigers in the phone book and I assume they were relatives, but we headed back to Germany with no success. It was great however seeing the area the Heinigers came from.

We concluded our trip with a couple of fun days in Munich. One of our favorite things was dinner at the Hofbrau House, a huge restaurant that has been serving food and drink continuously since some time in the thirteenth century; A great trip.

DURING OUR TIME IN Pennsylvania a number of family changes took place. Jon and Stephanie moved from Hawaii to California when Jon was assigned as Captain of a Cutter headquartered in Newport, just south of L.A. . His journey from a non practicing Catholic to a committed conservative Christian was amazing. His struggle was with the concept of Faith. He was trained as an Electrical Engineer so everything had a cause and effect. We put him in touch with Rich Aberle who I mentioned earlier. Rich was a nuclear engineer so he and Jon really clicked. Jon accepted Jesus Christ as his Lord and Savior and he was baptized outdoors in a fountain

Steph graduated from Baypath College before she married Jon and while they were in Hawaii she continued her studies at the University of Hawaii. She enrolled in Cal State Fullerton when they moved to California and got her bachelor's degree while they were there. I was very proud of her for completing her degree. It would have been easy to "not bother," especially since she had a baby and a husband that was not always around. After spending some time in California Jon was asked by the Coast Guard to move to Virginia and enroll in Law School at William and Mary. This was a great honor as well as a wonderful opportunity. While he was going to school he received his normal pay and his time counted for time in service. Three years later he graduated with honors.

While they lived in Virginia, Jon and Steph bought their first house and proceeded to fill it up. Katie was born on September 9, 1990, and Christian came along a couple of years later on July 29. The three years that they were in Virginia was the first time that we were relatively close and that allowed us to spend holidays and other events together. A trip to Hershey Pa. for our twenty fifth anniversary in 1989 was one fun family time. We had a number of great Thanksgiving and Christmas times together. After Jon completed his studies at William and Mary, he was assigned to work at the Coast Guard base on Governors Island just south of New York City.

A family tradition began during our time in Pa. We discovered the Outer Banks of North Carolina, specifically Nags Head. We rented a house for a week and enjoyed it greatly. A fun golf course and the beautiful beach within walking distance made for a perfect vacation. We also visited Kitty Hawk and the Wright Brothers museum. We returned many more summers and eventually rented a house for two weeks, one week for the whole family and one week for just Diann and me.

In March of 1996, David, Jon and I headed for the Grand Canyon. We had planned to take the trip in 1995 but mudslides closed the trails and it took months to restore them. We began our trip to the bottom of the canyon around noon. It was a cool clear day with some snow and ice along the trail at the top. The temperature was in the 50's.

The trip to the bottom was about twelve miles and it was a beautiful walk. From pine trees and snow at the top to ninety plus degrees and desert like conditions at the bottom, the beauty of the canyon kept our attention all the way. We arrived at the bottom of the canyon and soaked our feet in the Colorado River. The water was crystal clear and ice cold. We stayed in a "bunkhouse" with twelve bunks in a very small room. The facility was called Phantom Ranch and we enjoyed a wonderful steak dinner that evening.

About dark, we all hit the rack and while I slept great, David said that he heard some interesting noises coming from the bunks around him. We were up before dawn and were served an excellent breakfast. They gave us a nice meal to go and we were on our way out as soon as it was light. The trip was along a different trail so all the sights were new.

Twelve miles all uphill was a challenge. We all made it out by noon with only one problem. Somewhere on the way out, Jon "blew" out one of his boots. Fortunately it was near the end of the trip as the sole was flapping with each step. Diann accompanied us on the trip but she stayed at the top in the beautiful El Tovar Lodge.

We covered about twenty four miles in twenty four hours and I was sore for a few days, but it was a wonderful experience.

In September of 1996 I took my first trip to Japan. I went with nine others from the retail division to share our ideas with our Japanese counterparts. It was seven days with non-stop activities. I loved Tokyo and the culture there. We were hosted by several senior management guys who felt it was imperative that we have no spare time. When we checked in to our hotel the first day, we were given a small business card and told to put it in our wallet. It had the address and phone number of the hotel. We were told that if we got lost we could give it to a cab driver and thus get a ride back to the hotel. I soon understood why.

All signs were in Kanji, the Chinese symbols that have been adapted to mean Japanese words. While all Japanese students take English in school, very few are willing to try to speak it. Getting lost in an unfamiliar area would be bad news, hence the card in the wallet. After every long day of business we had a few minutes to relax and then we were "out for the night." Great food, entertainment, Geisha girls, etc. etc.

We rode a high speed bullet train to a factory about hundred miles from Tokyo. While on the train I experienced the Japanese skill of sleeping. Before the train had reached top speed every person in our car was asleep except, we Americans! They can and do sleep anywhere anytime. Many of them have commutes that take four to five hours a day so they sleep whenever and wherever they can.

After the plant tour we visited the "proving grounds" where we got to ride around a track in a car at very high speed. We saw the various tests that tires must go through before going into production. After about four or five nights out with Japanese cuisine, we were told, "tonight we were going to have a special treat." We were thinking steak or something western, but we boarded a bus and we soon arrived in Chinatown. What a treat! Our last day was a free day.

Bridgestone policy prevented us from all flying on the same plane so five of us got an extra day in Tokyo. We visited a beautiful garden, took a boat ride on a river, and visited the famous Ginza business district. Since we were on our own the last night we found a U.S restaurant, Damon's Ribs. What a treat. The trip home was the longest plane ride I have ever experienced. Fifteen hours nonstop from Tokyo to Atlanta, followed by a two hour flight to Philadelphia; it was an exhausting trip but a wonderful experience.

As stated earlier, the Northeast Zone consisted of two hundred sixty five stores when I took the assignment. During the next twelve years we began an aggressive campaign to increase our distribution. We opened a number of new locations, closed some "dogs" and purchased a number of facilities from dealers that wanted to sell out. We bought the J.C. Penny Auto Centers, purchased twenty one locations from a dealer in upstate New York and by 1996 the Northeast Zone had grown to three hundred thirty locations. I was pleased with the sales and profit progress the Zone had made.

By September of 1997, I had settled in and planned to spend the next few years wrapping up my career with the company. About a year earlier we decided to sell our big house and move to a new area nearby that was a planned community with shopping and restaurants within walking distance. We purchased a lot and started our new home. Our house sold quickly leaving us somewhat homeless for a few weeks. Diann flew to Hawaii to spend some time with the Beyer family. I was at a grand opening of a new store in the Philadelphia area on a Friday afternoon when I got a much unexpected phone call from my boss, Dave Luck. He told me that Bridgestone had just purchased a company in Miami Florida and that I had been selected as a possible candidate to become the president of the new division.

For the previous thirty years, Bridgestone had distributed their aircraft tires through a distributor, Thompson Aerospace. Thompson had a facility in Miami Florida where they warehoused new Bridgestone Aircraft tires and retreaded worn tires. Thompson, which was privately owned by one man who lived in France, had at one time been a strong and viable company but had "lost its way" and was losing market share each year. Bridgestone decided to buy the company and make it part of the Bridgestone family. Mr. Luck wanted to know if I was interested in interviewing for the assignment. I called Diann and asked her what she thought. After considering the pros and cons, I decided there was no harm in going for an interview.

A few days later I was asked to meet with two men from Bridgestone's Tokyo headquarters to discuss the assignment. They flew into Philadelphia and met me at a downtown restaurant. I immediately liked them both. One was "Kevin" Nomura and the other was "Rocky" Imura. Almost all Japanese businessmen take an English first name or "nickname" when they do business in the USA. Kevin was a Vice President of the parent Bridgestone company and Rocky was in charge of aircraft tire activity worldwide.

The interview went well and a few days later I was asked to fly to Nashville for a second interview. I learned that the new company would be responsible for all Aircraft Tire Activity in North and South America, the Caribbean and Guam. After that interview I was offered the job. The next day I flew to Miami and met with the man who was the President of Thompson and spent a day with him. He was to move to a Vice President position after the sale was finalized. While I did not go to the company headquarters, I did look around the area and liked what I saw.

Since I had a house under construction the move was a bit complicated. I negotiated a salary that would allow me to keep the house in Pa. and purchase a Town home in Florida. A nice car allowance and a membership at a country club sealed the deal. At that time my plan was to work for about five more years and then retire with a home in Pennsylvania for the summer and Florida in the winter. Diann had other ideas! More on that later.

CHAPTER 19

Sunny South Florida

I reported to Miami on October 1, 1997 and was introduced to the employees of Thompson Aircraft Tire. They were all told that they could keep their positions initially and that good performance would allow them to keep their jobs long term. After I was introduced by Rocky, he headed back to Japan. I met with the key people and took a tour of the facility. The company had about thirty five salaried people and about one hundred forty hourly. The tour of the plant and warehouse was demoralizing.

It was old, dark, dirty, and just depressing. It looked as if no money had been spent for years. The office was also in need of a lot of work. I soon found out that the culture was such that salaried people wandered into work from 8 AM until about 8:30. At 5:01 the place was vacant.

Some of the ladies dressed like they were going to a party rather than going to an office job. I asked the four VP's what the vacation policy was and got four different answers. No written policy manual existed. The last thing Rocky told me before he left was that my job was to "bring the company into the Bridgestone culture." Bridgestone was a typical Japanese company - detail oriented, disciplined, and focused on profitability. Thompson was none of the above.

I have stated many times since my time in Miami, "I either greatly underestimated the task ahead or greatly overestimated my ability to turn a company around." It was a tremendous challenge.

During the first few months we scrubbed the layers of grease off the floor in the plant, painted all walls, equipment, and everything else that did not move. The employee kitchen and break room was disgraceful so it was totally renovated. We improved the lighting and fixed a lot of safety issues. There was no security - anyone could walk into the building at a number of points. We secured the facility so employees had to use a card to enter the facility.

Only after all the improvements were made did we put the Bridgestone sign on the front of the building. We then invited all of our customers to a "Grand Opening" with a meeting in Miami Beach followed by a plant tour. The next four years consisted of continual improvement (one of the most used words in the Japanese language is Kaizen, which means continual improvement) of the facility and the operation of the company.

The plant employees came from dozens of countries from Central America, South America and the Caribbean. Only three or four were born in the U.S.A. About twenty five were from Haiti and they were my favorites. They were hard working, dependable and just sweet people. Most of their income was sent back to their homeland. Almost all plant employees stayed and thrived in the improved facility.

We provided uniforms, had contests, and focused on improvement every day. Safety policies did not exist and in fact an employee was killed at the plant less than a year earlier. He was carelessly using a solvent that was flammable and he was burned to death. With the help of the Manager of Corporate Safety for Bridgestone, we identified many items that needed to be corrected and got the plant into shape.

When we went ninety days without a lost time accident, I brought a grill and cooked hamburgers for all of the employees. The people on the second shift and the midnight shift were especially appreciative that I came back to cook for them. When we achieved six months with no lost time accidents I cooked steaks. There was a lot of peer pressure to make sure no one was hurt. There were no serious accidents during my time at B. A. U. (Bridgestone Aircraft Tire U.S.A.)

The Salaried employees were another story. About half of the original group were gone within a year, including two VP's. They just could not or would not adapt to the Bridgestone culture.

Most people are surprised to find out that the huge jet airplanes that we fly in are almost all running on retreads. Typically, aircraft tires are retreaded up to twelve times before they are scrapped. Only then is a new tire installed to replace the scrapped tire. The Miami Facility retreaded over one thousand tires a week. During my four plus years there, we had less than twenty tires fail, a tribute to the Bridgestone process and the quality control that is in place. We had a fleet of semi-trucks that delivered our products to all points in North America.

I returned to Pennsylvania late in November for Thanksgiving in our new home. Diann was teaching at Windsor Baptist Pre-School and she decided to finish out the year. From November until school was out in May she traveled to Miami about three times a month for a long weekend and I went back to PA. once a month. In May she moved to Miami and we only went back to Pennsylvania occasionally. David moved into our home in Pennsylvania.

That was a very difficult time for her, as she felt that she did not have a home. Once during that first year, I asked her how she was doing. She decided that it would be best to give me a word picture. We all are familiar with the pieces of tires that are seen along the highway. They are officially called tread separation or abbreviated as "tread sep." She told me that she "felt like one of those pieces of tread, constantly run over by cars and trucks." I got the picture. It was great when she finished her teaching responsibilities and spent all of her time in Florida.

Our Florida home was in Pembroke Pines, a relatively new city half way between Miami and Fort Lauderdale. "The Pines" was the third fastest growing city in the U.S.A. during the 90's going from a very small area to over one hundred thousand residents. It was a classic example of sprawl, with no real town but just shopping centers and housing developments for miles. It had Hollywood as an eastern border and the Everglades as a western border. We soon found out that no church buildings were there, but only congregations that met in schools, theatres, shopping centers etc. We tried several and settled in at the Church of the Pines, a church plant from First Baptist Church of Hollywood, a large thriving Baptist Church.

We thoroughly enjoyed our time at the Pines Church. It was made up of about one third white, one third black and one third Hispanic worshipers. We met in a double wide trailer which was our first permanent home after starting out in a theatre. During our time there, we built a permanent facility which seated about six hundred. We had a Saturday night service and after a couple of years in the new building we filled it on Sunday morning.

We visited there recently. There is still a Saturday night service and three on Sunday morning. The same pastor that was there when we moved there is still leading the congregation. God has surely blessed him and the church.

I WAS THE HEAD OF THE Usher/Greeter ministry and was in charge of the fundraising to build the new facility. Di was co-leader of Women's Ministry and led a bible study and counseled. One of the fundraisers was unique. The pastor gave everyone a crisp new one dollar bill as they left the sanctuary on a Sunday morning. He challenged us to see what we could turn it into in a month. It was just before we moved to N.C. so I will tell you in the next chapter what I did with my dollar.

I loved living in South Florida. The weather suited me, the variety of food and entertainment was great, I belonged to a nice Country Club paid by Bridgestone, and I had access to Doral, the famous Country Club in Miami where we had a corporate membership. Diann did not enjoy the summers as the heat is never ending. Most summer mornings it is eighty degrees by 6 AM and into the ninety's almost every day. From May to October the heat never lets up. Rain comes most afternoons followed by the sun which means steam. Winters are beautiful with most days in the seventy's with very little rain. I also enjoyed the culture of people from all over the western hemisphere. Our company with about one hundred sixty five employees had only about twenty of us who were born in the USA. The rest were from about twenty different countries and they spoke several different languages. All employees were required to speak English as The FAA required all communication to be in English, but it was interesting to hear the different languages and dialects in the break room.

While we were living in South Florida Diann and I decided to take the entire family on a trip to a Dude ranch in Arizona, Rancho de los Caballeros. Before heading west, I decided that I needed to do some riding as I had not been on a horse in years. I found a riding academy near our home and called and made an appointment. When I arrived I found myself in a strange situation. This academy taught English style riding. I am sure the girls chuckled when they saw me with my boots and jeans. I soon found myself on a horse going in a circle with a bunch of twelve year old girls. It was my first experience with an English saddle and I kept thinking I would go head first off of the horse and end up like Christopher Reeves, but I stayed for the entire lesson. I should have left when I realized was going on, but for some reason I stayed. Strange day!

Our trip to the ranch was great. In addition to great riding and great accommodations, there was a championship golf course on the ranch. Riding in the morning and golf in the afternoon great weather and delicious food - it doesn't get much better than that. Everyone had a great time. Unfortunately Dave could not make the trip, which was disappointing.

During my first year at B.A.U., I had a lot to learn. Almost none of my experience in "ground" tires translated to aircraft. We sold some tires, but most of the time we leased them. Customers were billed each month based on the number of landings they had. Almost all of our business was by five year contracts. Bidding was time consuming and stressful. Our customers were United Airlines, Boeing, American Airlines, Alaska Airlines, Aloha Airlines, and several smaller airlines, including several airlines that only handled freight. We had many good customers in South America and Canada as well, and the U.S. Navy and Coast Guard, and Marines were good customers as well.

In total, when I arrived we had only about 13% of the aircraft tire business in the Americas. I spent a great deal of time "on the road with my salesmen and VP of sales, calling on customers as well as the companies that we did not do business with. My goal was to convince them to consider Bridgestone when their next contract expired.

My greatest success story was the signing of Continental Airlines which had been a one hundred percent Goodyear customer. They had over four hundred aircraft and that made them one of our three biggest customers. Delta had been a one hundred percent Goodyear customer forever and we secured a small portion of their business also.

Bridgestone Factory in Japan

I FLEW A LOT OF MILES during my four plus years at B.A.U. Trips to Japan, Europe and South America were constant, as well as travel all over North America. One of my most memorable trips was to a small freight carrier, Evergreen Airlines. They were located in McMinnville Oregon and they operated a fleet of Boeing "747" aircraft that they used to move freight and troops all over the world. A few years earlier, they purchased the famous Spruce Goose which was a huge wooden plane built by Howard Hughes during World War Two. His vision was for the plane to haul troops and freight for the war effort. Diann and I toured the plane a few years earlier when it was kept in Long Beach California, but the tour only included a very small part of the plane and the cockpit.

When visiting Evergreen, I was invited to take a tour of the plane. It was awesome. It has eight engines with space for a mechanic to stand behind each one and a wingspan far bigger than any airplane flying today. It was made mostly of wood because of a shortage of metal because of the war. It only flew one time for a very short distance—and by the time it was ready to go, the war was over. Later, Evergreen Airlines went bankrupt but the "goose" is currently in a museum in McMinnville.

In June of 1999 Diann and I joined a group of folks from Pines Church and flew to Israel with our pastor and his wife. We spent eight days touring the Holy Land, walking where Christ walked and standing on the sites we had read about in the bible. What a life changing experience. Now when reading the bible we often can visualize exactly what the setting looks like. I highly recommend all Christians taking this trip when possible.

On January 4th, 2000 my mom, Esther Bucher passed away. She was eighty three years old. Until about eight or nine years earlier she lived alone and was in good health. We began to notice some changes when she was in her early to mid seventies that were concerning. She made some strange statements and appeared to be a bit paranoid at times. We eventually moved her to the Apostolic Christian Retirement home in Francesville, Indiana where she had a nice apartment. Her dementia progressed until the final few years when she had full blown Alzheimer's disease. Her last months were spent in a special Alzheimer's facility near Fort Wayne, Indiana. She did not know anyone, but seemed content and was in a great facility. Alzheimer's is a cruel disease that seems to be much too common lately. She was a great lady, a great Mom and is very much missed.

After the funeral, Diann and I visited my Uncle Ken. He informed me that he was retiring from farming and was having a farm sale later that spring. While looking at all of his farm equipment that was going to be sold, I spotted a small orange tractor in the corner of his shed. I asked if that was Grandpa's first tractor and he said that it was. When I asked if he was planning to sell it he said that everything was going to be sold including the 1937 Allis Chalmers. He told me that it had not run since about 1960 and it obviously needed to be completely rebuilt. It sat outside for many years. Sometime around 1990 Uncle Ken moved it into his machinery shed.

It was on a golf course in Florida that I learned what happened many years earlier in Cleveland when I was abruptly demoted and moved to Hartford. Larry Jordan was the guy who got promoted at that time to replace Paul Dolan, my counterpart in the Western U.S. Jordan later left the company.

When a group of us got together to play golf in Florida he asked me if I knew why I got demoted I said I did not and he then told me the story. It seems that Bob Bowen, the executive Vice President of Firestone at the time did not like Dolan. He told Larry Lombardo to get him off the job and it turns out Dolan's wife was a H.R. executive at some company and the fear was that he would sue. So, Bowen said OK, get Bucher also. So even though my performance was good, I became the scapegoat. When it happened, for about a week I was very unhappy, but I then decided to keep my chin up and dig in at Hartford. Jordan and Terry Sprott, the guy who replaced me both left the company, and Bowen was fired also. Ten years later I was a division president and all of the other people who were involved in that fiasco were gone. I did OK!

In early 2000, I was informed that Bridgestone was going to change their retirement policy as of Jan. 1, 2001. Up until that time, full retirement came at age sixty five. Your retirement pay was calculated by age and number of years service and for every year that you retired prior to age sixty five you were assessed a penalty. On Jan. 1, 2001 the policy changed to full retirement when your age and years of service totaled ninety two.

When I heard the news I was fifty seven and I had thirty six years of service, a total of ninety three. Since my life was largely spent on airplanes and in hotels all over North and South America, with an occasional trip to Europe and Japan, I decided that when I got to the spring of 2001 I would retire. Since we were in the process of installing an entirely new computer system that would integrate sales, accounting, manufacturing etc., and we were totally renovating our office building, I wanted to be sure both projects were on track and close to finish before I checked out. I left at the end of February and in 2000 our market share had grown to over twenty percent, a huge increase in four plus years.

THE DORAL RYDER OPEN is a PGA golf tournament that is played at Doral Country Club, in Miami, each spring. In 2000, I invited one of my customers, an avid golfer, to join me in the Pro-Am with two other customers of Bridgestone. The professionals are required to play Wednesdays before each golf tournament in a charity event. It consists of one pro and four amateurs. There were about sixty teams entered. The cost is twenty five hundred dollars per player which all goes to local charities. Only companies that have some connection to the tournament can enter a team. Bridgestone is a major supplier to Ryder plus they provided all of the balls on the driving range.

We all met on Tuesday night for dinner plus the drawing of the pros. My team drew Olin Browne. While he is not well known, he did win on the PGA tour four times before moving to the senior tour. We got hats, shirts, jackets and a bunch of other stuff just for entering.

Just before teeing off, Olin got us together and told us to ask him whatever we wanted, but not in his backswing. Just before we started he said, "Let's go win this thing." He turned out to be a joy to play with. He gave us tips and generally entertained us. The best ball of each team was counted. We ended up shooting fifty four and we tied for first place. We got a bunch of neat stuff for winning. It was probably the most fun I have ever had on a golf course. It was a bit nerve racking as there was quite a crowd on hand. Warming up on the practice green with pros all around was awesome. David flew down to be my caddy. It was a Great Day!

While the travel was tiresome, I was blessed to see a lot of the world that I otherwise would not have seen. I visited Japan several times, Belgium, the site of the battle of Waterloo, Chile, Argentina, Brazil and many places in the USA, Canada and Mexico.

My idea of a perfect retirement was to keep our townhouse in Florida and keep Florida as our primary residence. Florida has no income tax! We still had our membership to Whitford Country Club in Pennsylvania so summers in Pa. and winters in Florida seemed to be perfect. Di had other ideas. She wanted to have one permanent residence and she preferred Pa. Keeping two homes is a bit complicated and as a counselor she felt it essential to be in one place. Since I had no interest in living where a snow shovel is required, we decided to sell both homes and locate somewhere in the middle.

I made a spread sheet with ten locations in four states, Virginia, North Carolina, South Carolina and Georgia. We planned to visit these locations during our final year in Florida and select the one that suited us best. Our first visit was to Pinehurst, the golf Mecca in the central part of North Carolina. We quickly ruled that out as too much of a tourist location. Our second visits were to New Bern and Wallace, North Carolina, two more golf friendly locations.

We arrived in New Bern on Memorial Day weekend with plans to spend Saturday in New Bern, Sunday in Wallace and return to Miami on Monday. The rest is history! After a few hours in New Bern and Taberna, Diann said, "this is it." So with no due diligence we put a deposit on a lot and headed back to Miami. The other eight locations did not get a visit and on Jan 1, 2001 we began building our new home.

One sad note was that Stephanie and Jon were living in Williamsburg, about four hours north and we were looking forward to being close to them and the grandkids for the first time. While we were building our house, they got transferred to Alaska, a very long distance away. So much for more time with the grandkids!

The Pennsylvania home sold quickly and on March 1 we put the Florida Townhouse on the market. It also sold quickly and with the New Bern house not scheduled to be completed until June we were homeless. Good friends with a condo in Florida let us move in and stay there until our house was done. It was great.

On Memorial Day weekend of 2001, we took occupancy of our new house in New Bern. Our Pennsylvania furnishings had been in storage and they arrived quickly. The lady that bought our townhouse also bought most of the furnishings so that worked out well. Retirement Begins!

CHAPTER 20

North Carolina

Life in our new home was great. A super golf course with a golf cart in my garage was something I had always hoped for. Our new home was on a beautiful wooded lot of almost two acres. For the first time in thirty seven years I had unlimited free time. Golf, landscaping and getting the new house set up took all of my time for a few months.

A friend from Pennsylvania gave me two suggestions. One was to become a volunteer counselor with S.C.O.R.E., which is an organization dedicated to helping folks start new businesses. The second was ValuTeachers. That is an organization that works with school teachers and other school employees with retirement planning. The vehicle is the 403b plan which is the government employee equivalent to the 401k for private companies. To market this type of plan a North Carolina Health and Life Insurance license is required so I went to school and earned my license.

During the next two years I visited over twenty five schools in Eastern North Carolina and attended teachers meetings, which were usually held around 4 to 5 PM. The next day I went back to the school and met with teachers who wanted to discuss their retirement. I helped several hundred teachers and administrators set up 403b plans to supplement their state retirement plan. I also met with dozens of folks that wanted guidance in starting their own small business. Both of these were satisfying activities.

Shortly after moving to North Carolina, I put my plan in place to raise money for the new church facility in South Florida. I used my dollar to send a letter to a number of friends asking them to sponsor me in a golf event. My plan was to walk and carry my clubs for as many holes as possible and to get people to commit to send an amount for each hole. Many people responded and most committed to one dollar per hole. I am sure they thought I would complete thirty six holes or maybe forty five. I started at 7 AM before the course opened and by lunch time had completed thirty six holes.

Diann walked with me and she pulled the stick on each hole. I went out after lunch and completed eighteen more for a total of fifty four. She called it a day and I headed out again and made it to sixty three! I was done! We headed to Outback for dinner and I was so stiff, Di had to help me out of the booth when we were done. My calculations tell me that I walked about twenty four miles that day. I raised almost three thousand dollars for the Pines church; great memory.

When I retired I had been playing golf for about thirty years. With little time to practice and limited time to play, my scores made little improvement over the years. With time to practice and play, my scores improved steadily after moving to North Carolina. When I retired my handicap was thirteen. That means my average score was somewhere between eighty two and eighty eight. My handicap decreased steadily and by 2008 it was in the four to five range. That means my average score was seventy five to eighty.

One magical day in 2008, I played the round of my life. When I finished the scorecard read sixty eight, four strokes under par. I had five birdies and one bogie and the rest of the holes were par. I have had a couple of seventy twos and a bunch of seventy threes, and seventy fours, but never again have I been below par. Now at age seventy four my goal is to shoot my age! I have come close but as of this date I have not accomplished that goal. Maybe soon!

In 2008 the movie Bucket List was one of the leading films. A wealthy guy found out that he had a terminal illness and he made a list of things he wanted to do before he "kicked the bucket." While I have never made a list, I have thought of a few things that I would like to see or accomplish during my time here. When living in Connecticut I decided to save the score cards of every golf course I played. In addition to the courses I played during my free time, I had a number of opportunities to take my golf clubs or at least my golf shoes on business trips. Somewhere along the way I thought that it would be fun to try to play a round of golf in every state in the U.S. By the time I retired I had played in the vast majority of states and a number of foreign countries.

In 2014, I had played in all the states but five, and the good news is that they are all in the same area. So, Diann and I planned a trip to complete my goal. We flew to Colorado and played a round the day we landed. We then headed to Wyoming and played there the next day; Onto South Dakota followed by North Dakota. We finished the week with a round in Montana. Doesn't look too bad on the map, but we put a lot of miles on the rental car that week. We saw some great sights along the way, with the Battle of Little Big Horn being the best. It is an awesome place to visit. At present I have played three hundred and seventy five golf courses in eleven countries. My all time favorite is Pine Valley in New Jersey. Being very private it is difficult to get on. I had two opportunities to play there while living in Pennsylvania. It is annually voted the number one course in the world. Awesome!

I bought my 1949 Chevy pickup truck in March of 1989 for fourteen hundred dollars. It was in running condition, but as an old farm truck was basically worn out. I used it for the next seven years to go to the dump, haul junk etc. When I moved to Florida I parked it in an outdoor storage facility where it sat for the next four years. After we moved into our new home in North Carolina I decided to bring it here. I flew to Pennsylvania and went to the storage unit to see if it would start. Amazingly, jumper cables were attached and it started quickly. I drove it to a Firestone store to get a quick checkup and the next day I left Pennsylvania early in the morning and headed south. David followed me in his car and we took turns driving the old truck.

When I say we drove the truck, I mean we "drove" the truck! It was in rough shape and at no time could you relax. Fifty miles per hour was as fast as we could safely drive, and since the steering was very loose it needed constant attention. The brakes were not very good when it left the factory and they were terrible at this time. Needless to say we were very happy to arrive at our destination after a fourteen hour trip.

In 2008 I decided to sell it as it was just not safe to drive. Dave protested and suggested we get it restored as it had been in the family for a long time. I finally agreed and decided to make it as original as possible. Finding parts and getting many items rebuilt was a long task, and difficult at times, but was very rewarding.

The first guy I hired quit after a couple of years so I moved it to another body shop. The owner agreed to complete the restoration but about two years later died of lung cancer. His wife asked me to let her finish it and she did! A long saga, but eight years after we started it is completed and beautiful.

Before Steph and family moved to Kodiak, they spent a few days with us in N.C.

After church one Sunday, we went to the Pollock Street Deli for lunch. After we had finished the meal, there was a plate full of unwanted vegetables on the table. Onions and Banana peppers, tomatoes and lettuce were heaped on the plate. I asked my Grandsons who would like to earn fifty dollars. Caleb declined, but ten year old Christian decided to give it a go. He washed it down with several Dr. Peppers and he earned the cash.

Needless to say, Mom and Grandma were not pleased with me.

In July of 2002, Diann, David and I flew to Kodiak Island Alaska to spend some time with Jon, Steph and the grandkids. It was a fun trip and we did a number of things that will be long remembered. After the long trip to Anchorage, Diann and I took the train to Denali for two days. We visited Mount McKinley and had a wonderful view of the mountain. The train was awesome and the scenery on the trip was amazing. What a beautiful part of the world. We did have a tough time sleeping as it never got totally dark.

Before heading to Kodiak, we played a round of golf at a great course on the Elmendorf Air Force base. We were teamed up with a neat guy who helped us navigate the course and who gave us some information on the area. Golf actually only lasts about four months a year, but the good news is that since it stays light until about 11 PM in the summer time, golf after work is no problem. Many folks tee off after 6 PM and have no trouble getting in eighteen holes.

We then flew to Kodiak and landed at the local airport which is a frightening experience. At one end of the runway is the ocean and at the other end is a mountain. Many flights are cancelled because of the often inclement weather on Kodiak Island. Shortly after arriving at their home, a very loud roar occurred just outside their house.

Looking out the window, I saw the wing of a C130 cargo plane taxiing by the house. It appeared to be less than one hundred feet from the house. Amazing!

While at Kodiak, we did a number of fun things. David and I flew on a pontoon plane to a remote lake over an hour from Kodiak. After we landed, the pilot took a rifle from behind his seat and told us to stay close to him. We walked on a pathway for about a quarter of a mile to a pond with a waterfall from the lake.

The goal was to see bears and we saw bears! Kodiak bears are the largest bears in the world. Males can grow to over ten feet tall and can weigh over seventeen hundred pounds.

We stopped on a ridge looking down on the pond, and saw many bears. For over an hour, we observed grown bears, and young bears fishing in the pond. Salmon are abundant in Alaska and this pond was no exception. It was amazing to watch the bears reach into the water and pull a big fish out of the water. One female had two cubs that appeared to be about half grown at her side. She pulled out a big fish. She tore it into two pieces and gave them to the cubs. Both flights were uneventful, but it did feel good when we landed on the water back at Kodiak.

WE ALSO WENT HORSEBACK riding. In addition to an abundance of fish, bald eagles are everywhere. Hundreds were spotted in a valley while on our ride. We also climbed the mountain that was at the end of the runway. It did not look too bad from the bottom, but it took several hours to reach the top. It was a difficult climb for old guys who did not have the correct shoes. The view was awesome but the trip down was almost as difficult as the climb. I was so sore the next day that every step was very painful. Jon, Steph, Dave, Caleb and I did the climb. Di stayed at the house with Kate and Christian.

We had not been home for many days when we got a call from Steph asking for prayer for Jon. He had suffered a seizure and they were testing him to determine the cause. After several weeks they determined that he had a brain tumor and he was given about one year to live. After a surgery and a move to San Francisco for a short time, the Beyer family relocated to New Bern.

Jon was an amazing person. His faith in Christ and his love for his family overshadowed his medical condition. Jon passed away later that year, a short time after he was the best man for David's wedding.

Seemed like he had determined to make it to the wedding and after it was over was ready to meet his Lord and Savior.

Di often remarks that she thinks of him everyday - he was a great man, a super father and husband and he is missed.

After Jon's death, David decided to relocate to North Carolina permanently. We both got our health and life insurance licenses. David worked as a Long Term Care Agent. He thoroughly hated the cold calling and decided quickly that he was not built to be an insurance agent. As I mentioned earlier, I called on schools and sold 403-b annuities.

Sometime in 2004, Dave suggested that we consider opening a tire and service store. While I had not planned to go into business, it was an intriguing idea. He commented that there was not one nice tire and service center in the area and that with all the growth in our area it would be a good fit.

Stephanie had some funds to invest from Jon's insurance so we began the journey. We searched for an appropriate existing facility and when we could not find one, we contacted a developer and began the process of building a new store. Since it was truly a family business, we named it Family Tire & Auto Service. Diann came up with our slogan -—We keep you rollin'.

After a long and sometimes painful journey building and equipping the store, we finally opened for business in November of 2005. The famous race car driver Mario Andretti came to our grand opening. We had some bumps in the road, but we persevered and by the third year we were making a nice profit.

Myself with Mario Andretti

IN 2008 WE OPENED OUR second store in Morehead City and in 2012 our third in Jacksonville. In 2010 Stephanie decided to exit the business so David and I became the owners. We currently employ about forty six teammates in the three stores. My role is primarily recruiting, marketing and training. I still enjoy working in a store one or two days a week. We have certainly been blessed during the past twelve years of owning small businesses.

When we moved to North Carolina our family consisted of eight people; Diann, Me, Dave, Jon, Steph, Caleb, Kate, and Christian. A lot has changed since then. First, Hope Stauffer moved from Pennsylvania. She and Dave were married at Temple Baptist Church. It was a beautiful fall day and the reception was held in our yard.

The next year, May of 2005, I heard that Kimmey Seymore's wife Natalie had died unexpectedly from an aneurism. Kimmey had been our dentist for several years and I also knew him from Little League baseball where we were both coaches. That fall Stephanie called me and asked me if I would coach a basketball team in the local youth league. I agreed to do so and soon after I participated in a draft session to select players. Of course I selected Christian first and then Sasha Seymore, Kimmey's son second. We had very little talent beyond the two big guys, but we had a great season and finished first in our league.

Soon after the season ended, Kimmey called Steph and invited her to lunch. More lunches followed and on October 14, 2006 they were married. Kimmey had four boys, so instantly Steph went from mom of three to mom of seven. Noah, Sasha, Jackson and Chase were now part of our family. Chase was only two when they married so it was a big adjustment for her. The family now numbered thirteen.

After Stephanie and Kimmey married, the family continued to grow. Noah married Maja, Katie married Taylor Andersen and Caleb married Evan. Two beautiful great grandsons, Luka Seymore and Aidan Andersen brought the total family to eighteen.

All of the adult kids are doing great. Jackson is a sophomore at the University of North Carolina and Chase is in the eighth grade.

In September 2008 Hurricane Ike hit Texas. While not as famous as Katrina, Ike made a huge impact on the coast of Texas north of Galveston. A few weeks after Ike hit, a group of men from Temple Baptist Church headed for the gulf. Jack Bender and his son Jake are contractors who employ about six men. They drove two trucks and trailers full of tools as well as their employees to the gulf. I decided that two days on the road each way was not good use of my time so I flew.

We spent a week replacing the roof on a Baptist church and a house owned by the church. I spent eight hours on the roof replacing shingles. It was hard work, but very satisfying. Mid week we got on a bus and toured the area. The devastation was amazing. Along the coast there was a twenty mile strip of land where every house was totally gone - just foundations left.

I would estimate that it was five hundred or more. Across the street, all of the rubble was in a lake of water. We slept on air mattresses on the floor of a Baptist Church nearby. The church ladies provided great food every morning and night and lunch was brought to us also. The people were so thankful for our service.

Our constant moving and my business travel have prevented me from doing much in the way of community service. Politics have always interested me but I have never had a big desire to run for political office. In 2009 I was approached by a local influential member of the Republican Party. He asked me to consider running for Alderman in the City of New Bern. New Bern is divided into six Wards with an Alderman for each ward. In addition there is a Mayor so that any vote cannot be a tie. The Board of Aldermen makes the laws and hires a full time City Manager to handle the day to day operations of the city. So, I filed the necessary papers and began the process.

While the positions of Alderman and Mayor are non-partisan, everyone knows who the Dems and who the Republicans are. I ran against a Democrat by the name of Max Freeze. He had been in office over twenty years and I think people were weary of him. A third candidate was Tony Bonnici, who wasn't much of a threat. I spent quite a bit of time campaigning and a bit of money for signs and TV spots. The whole family was involved and all worked to help me. When it was over I won with over seven hundred votes. Freeze and Bonnici together got just over three hundred.

The next four years were interesting. Four Democrats and three Republicans meant a number of issues did not go my way. As a board however, we did accomplish a number of goals and I believe we moved the city in a very positive direction.

In 2013 when my four years were up I had a decision to make. Run again for Alderman, retire from the board, or run for Mayor. I decided to run for Mayor. There were five other candidates in the race. The winner must get over fifty percent of the vote or there is a runoff in November. I hired a campaign manager, made TV spots and knocked on hundreds of doors.

The result was not what I had hoped for. I finished third. The new Mayor was a Democrat who had been on the board with me for the previous four years. He grew up here and his father had been the City Manager here years ago. That ended my political career and while I would have enjoyed being the Mayor, during the past four years I have often given thanks that I did not have to put on a suit and tie and endure long meetings.

EVERY AUGUST FOR THE past fifteen years or so, I have traveled to Toledo, Ohio to join a group of guys from Valpo for four days of golf. These are guys who grew up together and have met for thirty or more years for golf and storytelling. Attendance has been as many as eighteen and as few as eight as the ranks have thinned over the years. Illness, injuries and death have taken their toll. We don't hit it as far or as straight as we once did, but it is always a fun time.

Jim Loyaza was in our wedding party and we have stayed in touch over the years. In 2010 at Toledo he told me that he had just done an amazing feat. He joined a group of people who road their bikes across Iowa. It is called RAGBRAI, the oldest, largest organized bike ride in the world. It was started by a reporter from the Des Moines Register newspaper over 35 years ago who decided to ride across the state getting stories from the small towns he rode through. A few of his readers joined him and the thing began. It grew each year and after a few years the decision was made to make it an official event and fundraiser. It is limited to the first ten thousand riders who register each year and pay several hundred dollars for the privilege of riding about five hundred miles in a week. Locals join the ride and some days the total is estimated to be over twenty thousand riders. Each day the ride is from fifty to ninety miles and stops in a town that is prepared for a mob. Concerts every night, food served in every church and food trucks are everywhere. Jim said it was a blast and I agreed to join him the next year. I bought a road bike and began preparing months before the ride.

The last week of July 2011 we began at the western border of Iowa. It is not a race but a survival event. First of all, I had no idea Iowa was so hilly. The route changes each year and 2011 was in the very southern part of the state which has no flat areas - just hills. Jim's wife drove the support car and took our gear, clothes and air mattresses to the next town each day. We usually slept in basements. The people were very friendly and getting a hot shower was wonderful. Each morning they provided breakfast and we had many great conversations with local folks.

July 2011 was very hot with temps in the nineties each day. After the second day, Jim dropped out. He just could not take the heat and hills. His daughter was with us also and she and I soldiered on. Jim joined us on the last day as we made it to the Mississippi river. Jim vowed to get into shape for the next year and we prepared to do it again.

In 2012 we again headed east from the Iowa state line the last week of July. As the route changes each year, we were a bit farther north but still in a lot of hills. It happened again! Jim dropped out after a couple of days and his daughter and I rolled on. I finished again but decided that it was probably better left to younger folks. It was a great experience described by someone as a State Fair on wheels. I still enjoy riding my bike but in a much more leisurely manner.

Our faith has been an integral part of our life for many years. When we moved to New Bern we attended Temple Baptist Church for about ten years. There I served as a Deacon, an adult Sunday school teacher and headed up the Usher/Greeter ministry. Diann taught a bible sturdy and served as a counselor to a number of women and married couples. In 2010 we transferred our membership to Tabernacle Baptist Church in downtown New Bern. There we are involved in similar activities. Diann and I both lead bible studies, and I teach an adult Sunday school class. I just concluded a four year term as a Deacon and now I am in charge of the Men's Ministry. We have many great friends there and it is especially nice to be able to walk to church.

May of 2014 was a memorable month. On a Friday evening Diann and I joined our neighbors and friends, Don and Lynn Rogers for a prime rib dinner at Taberna C.C. I dropped them off at the door and parked my truck. When I got out of the truck, something did not feel right. I was nauseous, I began to sweat and generally felt terrible. I headed for the club and by the time I got to our table, I felt better. I wasn't sure what had happened, but decided to ignore it. I ate dinner and felt fine until later that evening when it happened again. I told Diann and she suggested a trip to the emergency room. I declined, took a couple of Tums and went to bed. Saturday morning we went to Capt'n Rattys and had breakfast.

Shortly after, it happened again. We went to the hospital and tests began. It was determined that I had a mild heart attack and I was admitted. A heart catheterization was scheduled for Monday morning.

The test revealed a total blockage of the artery below the heart, a condition that is known as the "widow maker."

A stent was installed to open the artery and I was released on Tuesday. One very interesting fact from my Cardiologist was that as the artery closed, my body "grew" several veins that bypassed the blockage. He said that if I had not been doing regular exercise, I probably would not have survived. Further tests showed no damage to my heart. Praise the Lord. My doc suggested I become a vegetarian, but he said he doubted I would do that. His then recommended only fish and chicken - a total of five times a week.

In September of 2015, I again felt something in my chest that did not feel normal. A stress test revealed some abnormality so back to the hospital for another heart cath. The blockage had reoccurred and another stent was installed. I have had no problems for the past two years and at a recent routine visit with my cardiologist, he said I am doing fine.

In the summer of 2016 I was invited to become a Gideon. I am sure you have seen Gideon placed Bibles in Hotels and Motels. . We also pass them out at schools and colleges, festivals and fairs. In addition, Gideon's and their wives place bibles in Hospitals, Nursing homes, and Doctor and Dentist offices. We provide Bibles to the military, policemen and firemen as well.

Last year we passed out more than ninety million scriptures in over one hundred languages. To raise funds to pay for the bibles, some Gideons go to local churches to ask for donations. In the past year, I have gone to six churches. Most Pastors will give us five to ten minutes to make the appeal. One Pastor told me the entire service was mine so I preached the sermon. It is a great ministry and countless lives have been saved by Bibles placed by Gideons.

It is now 2017. In January of 2015 Diann and I along with our friends Steve and Sabrina Bengel bought a four story brick office building in downtown New Bern. It was built in 1924 and for many years was a privately owned office building occupied by lawyers, architects, and other offices. In the 1980's it was purchased by the city of New Bern where it housed the Human Resources Dept., the Development Department, the tax and permit departments, etc. It took almost one year to complete the process of turning the building into condominiums. In January of 2016 we sold each condo. Diann and I bought the fourth floor and had it completely gutted.

In April we started the process of making it into our home. It is twenty six hundred square feet and has great views in all four directions. Our home in Taberna sold quickly and we had to move into a rental house for about a year. Our move into our downtown condo makes our seventeenth residence in our fifty three years of marriage. God willing this will be our final residence here on earth. .

The process was completed on November 1 and we moved in on Election Day and celebrated President Trump's election in our new home. We can now walk to Church, the post office, the hardware store, dry cleaners, bank and about twenty restaurants, as well as many other stores and shops.

Largely because of my career, I have been blessed to travel all over the world and have met a lot of famous people.

Here are a few.

Mario Andretti—Race Car Driver. Earlier this decade, he was voted the greatest auto race driver of the 20th century. I met him several times during my years with Firestone and he attended the grand openings of all three of our Family Tire Stores. He is truly a gentleman who never tires of shaking hands and signing autographs.

Mike Huckaby—former Governor of Arkansas, Fox News host and two time candidate for US President. He was a very nice man, interested in what I did.

Jimmy Carter—When he was Governor of Georgia my customer, Georgia Senator Paul Braun invited me to the Governor's office to meet Mr. Carter. He seemed a bit distracted, but had pictures taken with me and sent them to me later. Little did I know then that he would soon announce his candidacy for President.

Charles Krauthammer—Fox News contributor and author. Diann and I had a short meeting with him prior to a speech he made here in North Carolina. Unlike his serious persona which we see on TV, he was warm and funny.

Newt Gingerich—Former Speaker of the House was here for a fundraiser for a local candidate. He was much more interested in talking to Diann than me.

Bob Dole—Nice man. We spent some time with him when his wife Elizabeth was U.S. Senator for North Carolina.

Charles Colson—Famous as President Nixon's lawyer during the Watergate debacle; I met him just before he spoke to thousands of men at a Promise Keeper event in NYC. His ministry was and is Prison Fellowship. He was kind, humble and took no credit for the fine work of his ministry. I was privileged to have met him.

Mike Didka—Hall of Fame football player and head coach of the Chicago Bears when they won their only Super Bowl. I was blessed to sit by him at lunch in Chicago as he was a spokesman for Firestone at the time. Very nice man - only wanted to talk about other people.

Raymond Floyd—Professional Golfer. Has a reputation for being a jerk. Agree!

Stan Musial—Hall of fame baseball player and great guy. I wrote about my meeting with him earlier.

Walter Payton—Hall of Fame running back for the Chicago Bears. His nickname as a Football player was "Sweetness." It also describes him as a person. He was a genuine nice man who died way too soon.

John Calipari—I met him when he was the head coach of the U Mass basketball team. Currently he is head coach of Kentucky. Not someone I am fond of but in my brief encounter with him he was very friendly.

Bill Walton—Hall of Fame Basketball Player. I was on an elevator in the Dallas Fort Worth Airport when he strolled on. While we were going down to the concourse he looked at me and said and I quote. "Can you believe how bad the Chicago Bulls are? You are better than some of the guys on that team." He then walked off the elevator and headed for his gate. He has a reputation for being a bit strange and he showed me that it is real and deserved."

Doug Collins—NBA all star and Coach. When Diann and I went to the 1984 Olympics as guests of Sports Illustrated, Doug was one of our hosts. We sat by he and his wife at an Olympic Basketball game. At the time David was playing High School Basketball and Doug was very helpful and kind to explain how to help him pick a college.

Jimmy Vasser—Not exactly a household name but anyone who is/ was interested in Indy Car racing will know the name. He was a championship driver and now is a car owner. I met with him several times and road with him in a Corvette on a track one time; scary but fun.

Scott Pruitt—Another famous race car driver. In 1995 Firestone re-entered Indy Car racing after a number of years absence. Scott was chosen to drive the only car that was on Firestone tires that year and he won the Michigan 500 race. Within a couple of years all Indy Cars were on Firestone. I attended a number of company events with Scott and he was a gracious and fun guy.

Bobby Rahal—Yet another Indy Car driver and now team owner. Bobby won the Indy 500 and many other races. After his race career was over, I was privileged to play a round of golf with him at his golf club, The Country Club in Columbus Ohio; another very nice man.

Tiny Tim —Tiny Tim (his real name was Herbert Khaury) was an entertainer who often appeared on the Tonight Show with Johnny Carson. He was famous for the song "Tiptoe through the tulips." I was on an elevator in a hotel in Hartford Connecticut when he walked on. I knew immediately who he was, but I said, "You look familiar." He said "I'm Tiny Tim." and I replied "no that's not who I thought you were, playing with him. He looked puzzled and got off on the next floor.

As a Bridgestone Firestone Employee and Customer, I have attended many events and met a number of well known and successful sports figures. Most of these meetings were very brief, often just time for a photo.

Some of them were:

Cal Ripken Jr.—Hall of Fame Shortstop

Don Shula—Miami Dolphins Coach

Lee Trevino—Champion Professional Golfer

Bob Griese—Hall of Fame quarterback

Joe Morgan —Hall of Fame baseball player

A C Green —LA Lakers star and devout Christian

James Worthy—LA Lakers star and member of Hall of Fame

Bobby Unser—Indy car driver - winner of three Indy 500 Races and many other races

Al Unser—Younger brother of Bobby - winner of four Indy 500 races and many other races

Finishing a 10-K run

Las Vegas Speedway – Top Lap 136

White Water Rafting - Pennsylvania

Bringing Bob Brainard's Sailboat from Florida to North Carolina

Coaching Temple Baptist Little League

Enjoying the Indy 500 with friends

Made in the USA
Columbia, SC
03 May 2018